Hal A. Huggins DDS, MS

 Dragon Slayer Publications

Copyright © 2004
by Hal A. Huggins DDS, MS

All rights reserved, including the right to reproduce this work in any form whatsoever, without permission in writing from the publisher, except for brief passages in connection with a review.

Illustrations by Casey Koester

For information write:

Hal A. Huggins DDS, MS
5082 List Drive
Colorado Springs, CO 80919

Or call: 1-866-948-4638
FAX: 1-719-548-8220

e-mail: email@hugnet.com
www.DrHuggins.com

ISBN 0-9724611-2-4

Other books
by Hal A. Huggins DDS, MS

It's All In Your Head

The Link Between Mercury Amalgams and Illness: Written in nontechnical, easy-to-understand language, this book explodes the claim that mercury amalgams are safe. Read about the research on mercury toxicity that the dental establishment has systematically ignored. Learn about the effects of mercury toxicity including MS, Alzheimer's, Hodgkin's and Chronic Fatigue. If you think your worries are all in your head, you may be right. The lower third.

Uninformed Consent (with Thomas E. Levy MD, JD)

The hidden dangers in dental care: Presents cases of toxic poisoning—of depressed immune systems and inexplicable illnesses—all easily traceable to the toxins leaching into the bloodstream from the heavy metals in dental materials. Find out the hidden truths that the dental industry in America doesn't want to talk about, and the *real* reasons the dangers of these materials have been suppressed and ignored.

Solving the MS Mystery

Help, Hope and Recovery: Based on 33 years experience of treating patients, Dr. Huggins shows that toxic dental materials in the mouth so close to the brain can trigger many autoimmune diseases including MS, Alzheimer's, Lupus, and Chronic Fatigue. Learn the Protocol that has worked to reverse these and other autoimmune diseases. Take charge of your health and become educated about treatments that work.

Your Goose Isn't Cooked-Yet!

A cookbook / nutrition book with over 230 recipes plus Mini-Chapters that reveal **Huggins' Secrets** —information usually given only during his body chemistry lectures—about carbohydrates, protein, salt, fish, grains, honey, fruits, etc. Learn the functions of blood, dental decay and degenerative disease. Get nutrition, meal planning and cooking tips that will help you balance your own chemistry and have fun in the kitchen.

Acknowledgements

*To those who helped transform
my thoughts into a book.*

First, of course, is to Dr. Melvin Page, who introduced me to the concept of the Androgynic Factor. Coming from the strictly chemistry standpoint, I'm not sure how he would feel about my expansion into the world of fun with people .... but he was a tolerant old andric, and maybe he will understand that all andrics have to put their own signature onto a new concept.

Second is to my Comma-Kazies. Donna Hedden and Patty Boone together deleted 8 million commas, added 8 million commas, but – they are not the same 8 million. They saw to it that my irreverences were sometimes converted to politically correct commentaries, but, thankfully, not all the time.

Donna Hedden also gets a second medal for her typesetting and formatting skills. She also puts up with my morning routine of, "Oh, by the way, Donna, here are some changes I would like to see incorporated." She does have too much fun with the creativity she adds to the volume. For that she will get — another book to assemble.

Next, there are the literally thousands of people wandering the planet that I have observed (unknowingly by them) who taught me by their actions that there are Androgynic Factors working every moment of every day in all of our lives.

Then, there is artist primo, Casey Koester. What a delightful fellow. You can see his real personality in his drawings. He gave me the fun of seeing my verbal requests magically converted into my favorite method of expression – line drawings. He also added a new dimension to friendship, to sharing, to appreciation for each other's skills. I have valued working with him and sharing his soul.

Illustrated by Casey Koester

Illustrator Casey Koester, retired art director, space salesman and creative consultant, comes from Cleveland, Ohio, having attended the Cleveland School of Art, John Huntington Polytech Institute and Landon School of Cartooning.

He served 4 1/2 years in World War II in Texas, California, the South Pacific, the Philippines and Japan. In fall 1945, he was on one of the first troop carriers that landed to occupy Japan where he became first cartoonist for the newly formed *Tokyo Stars & Stripes* newspaper.

He has been art director of TV and sales promotions, working for BBDO (Batten, Barton, Durstin and Osborn) Advertising Agency, and the Meldrum and Fewsmith Advertising Agency in Cleveland.

He returned to Colorado Springs in 1994. Here he has produced three art exhibits with local professional artists participating. Casey also paints watercolors and acrylics. He has painted five murals at the Village at Skyline retirement center using ordinary waterbase house paint.

As a freelance artist, Casey has a wondrous ability to turn concepts into cartoons and ideas into images – all with a delightful sense of humor.

Dedication

After many years   of soft persuasion
Many months   of active threats
Many weeks   of logication
What Patty wants   Patty gets

This book has simmered   in my head
From rising up   to seeking bed
With Patty's pushing   I succumb
To show you why   Your Hormones Hum

Dedicated to:
Dr. Patty MacDonald Boone

Table of Contents

Hormonal Basis of "Love" 1
Introduction to the Turmoil of a New Discovery 2
Background for Biological Attraction 3
The Hormonal Fascination 22
Pre-Marriage Predictions 25
Graphic Examples 30
How Does the Other Half Live? 39
The Big Guns – Estrogen and Testosterone 43
Andric *** Gynic 48
    Andric - Gynic Habits? 51
    General Characteristics 53
    Show *** and *** Tell 58
    Business *** Occupation 63
    Secure *** Insecure 80
    Abrasive *** Conciliatory 88
    Active *** Passive 90
    Vacations 95
    Creativity *** Organization 99
    Fast Food *** Dining 102
    Call for the Psychologist 108
    Dress Codes 113
    Sports 115
    In Sickness *** and *** In Health 116
    Perplexing Habits 123
    Let Me Entertain You 128
    Offense *** Defense 131
    What Are Your Chances? 134
    Identification – What Are You?
        Andric *** or *** Gynic? 135
Oscillating Hormones 143
Living Happily Ever After 147

Preface

This book is about hormones. More specifically, it is about how your hormones guide your daily decisions, and how the reflections between your hormones and someone else's determine how your personal interrelationship with that person will develop. Friendships, dating, marriages, working relationships – any situation in which you have to interact with another person – are dependent upon how your (and the other person's) hormones interrelate – even if you never touch.

The strongest influence we feel in emotional reactions between males and females is produced by estrogen and testosterone. The guidance system controlled by estrogen is termed "<u>Gynic</u>" (pronounced gen-ick) -- derived from the same root word as gynecology. Its equal and opposite driving force is testosterone dominance, called "<u>Andric</u>" (pronounced an-drick). This comes from the word androgen, or male household. Surprisingly, andric and gynic behavior appears 50-50 in both males and females. Only at the polar ends of the definitions do the terms reflect the lion behavior of the andric and lamb behavior of the gynic. Both sexes manufacture both hormones, and both sexes are influenced by minute increases or decreases of these hormones. Hormone levels eventually control every human interaction we experience every day.

Hormones are tiny chemicals produced by your endocrine glands. Endocrine glands by name include your thyroid, parathyroid, pituitary, pancreas, ovaries, testes, adrenal, parotid and probably others we don't even know about. By weight, these tiny chemicals are more powerful than atomic bombs, so it doesn't take many molecules to create a major effect on your biological and social functions.

An extreme case of physical hormonal influence is the story we have all heard about 95 pound Granny who picks up a grand piano and carries it out of a burning house. That is adrenalin. Your adrenals and all your other hormone-producing endocrine glands shape your day – all day – every day.

Hormonal Basis of "Love"

Remember the first time you fell in love? Maybe you were ten years old. You looked, and he/she looked back. You both blushed and examined your shoelaces. Your heart fluttered. You got a lump in your throat. Later you asked your Mom, "What is love?" You *really* wanted to know, because you had just experienced a jambalaya of unfamiliar emotions and didn't know how to explain them. Was this love?

Did Mom give you a satisfactory answer? Probably not. Something about, "you'll know", or "you are too young", or the prime cop-out, "ask your Father". Brother, like he knew anything about love. It probably sounded like an intellectual issue beyond your ability to understand. Yet, it was *you* that had this unique experience, and, whatever it was, you knew it was real. You just didn't have the vocabulary to express it.

> *What you are experiencing is that innate attraction that continues the species.*

Well, actually, most people never develop a satisfactory vocabulary in this arena because what you are experiencing is not a verbal thing. It is hormonal. It is that innate attraction that continues the species. You just had a biochemical experience. **Someone made your hormones hum.** You felt it disguised as an emotion, but, bottom line, it is simply the way life continues itself on this planet. It is biological genetics, not something you can read about in a book — until now.

Introduction to the Turmoil of a New Discovery

In the introduction to one of Dr. Weston Price's books, he paraphrased 19th century chemist Liebig in saying, "A New Truth – A New Sense." I will further paraphrase by both expanding Price and then condensing the rather extensive commentary by Liebig.

> *"The acquisition of a new truth is like the acquisition of a new sense. It allows man the capability to perceive and recognize new phenomena that were invisible and hidden from him originally."*

I was first introduced to the Andric-Gynic concepts disclosed in this book as a side issue of learning how to balance body chemistry to achieve better oral and systemic health. What I learned was that in addition to this, my grand-mentor Dr. Melvin Page had disclosed to me the secret of human personal interaction. We all look at life through our own lenses, and see it differently, but, there are *reasons* for these differences. It is not just that those people are cantankerous. Through these studies, I learned that probably nothing is right or wrong. Just different interpretations of the same event by different people – dependent upon how their endocrine glands are influencing their decisions.

| This is genetics as an entirely New Truth. |

This is genetics as an entirely New Truth.

Background for Biological Attraction

Page's work in nutrition, endocrinology, dentistry and psychology pulls together many of the pieces of the health puzzle that have been lost by separation into individual sciences. This situation was well stated by the former chairman of the Executive Council of the United Nations' Food and Agriculture Organization. Jose de Castro stated,

> *"The tremendous impact of scientific progress has produced a fragmentation of culture and pulverized it into little grains of learning. Each scientific specialist has seized his granule and turned it over and over beneath the powerful lens of his microscope, striving to penetrate its microcosm, with marvelous indifference to and a towering ignorance of everything around him."*

I feel that this grain of endocrinology supplied by Dr. Page can be a valuable lesson to all of us in better understanding ourselves and others, and – in particular – how we interact.

"Biological attraction" between male and female is not just for mate selection. It can be used by everyone who deals with other human beings, be it subjective or objective.

| *Biological attraction between male and female is not just for mate selection.* |

The *subjective* portion, or the non-objective, vapor-ware type "feelings" described in this book are experienced *across the sex line.* That is, male to female, and female to male. Who Makes Your Hormones Hum? explains how to use identification of hormonal patterns in both cases – subjective and objective. *Subjective* is what some people call "vibes" - "animal magnetism"

- "soul mates" - "non-verbal communication" — the ethereal interactions that we all know are there, but cannot put our finger on.

Same sex human interaction is more based on intellectual and mutual interest subjects that are *objective*. We can *see* the results of interaction visibly. We can describe them verbally. As an example, we will buy / not buy the objective automobile sitting in front of us on the objective car lot. But! If the transaction is from a person of one sex to another sex, there will be the addition of another part of the decision based on how our *subjective* hormones drive our decision-making process. Those across the sex line hormonal decisions to buy can be swayed by the opposite sex salesperson.

Understanding what drives the subjective side of people does give one the advantage in knowing how to communicate our ideas to another person. For when we understand "what makes people tick" (their hormones), we can better determine how to present material to them that we want to be understood.

> *I treat two women exactly the same way, say exactly the same things, and one accepts me, supports my ideas, while the other rejects both me and my ideas.*

Subjective interpretation of hormone interactions explains why you get along socially with some people of the opposite sex, and are not able to tolerate others for more than ten seconds. Men frequently admit to not being able to understand women in either business or social settings. Is this *all* women, or does it just seem like it? It may just be those of the same endocrine pattern.

"I treat two women exactly the same way, say exactly the same things, and one accepts me, supports my ideas, while the other rejects both me *and* my ideas."

The difference is that the two women are of totally opposite hormone patterns. One conversation makes both of you hum, the other is discordant. It's not you; it's the hormone match that counts.

These interactions are not always – in fact – are <u>never</u> under your control. You may learn how to avert disaster by understanding the hormonal dynamics of human interaction and learn how to skirt around sensitive issues gracefully, but the underlying feelings are dictated by your genetics and are not subject to change.

Take the case of Sam and Janet. Remember the song? Sam sees Janet across a crowded room and immediately falls in love with her. The song was titled something like "Sam and Janet Evening". Now, the great thing was that Janet felt the same way about Sam at the same time Sam felt that way about Janet. They soon discovered they were "soul mates". Soul mates simply means that you have found someone with all the endocrine patterns equal and opposite to yours. Logic has nothing to do with it. It is who makes your hormones hum.

In one segment of MASH, Hawkeye sees an old girl friend drive into camp. He immediately flips out. They had been engaged at one time, but she had turned him down because he was already married to his profession. She wanted a homebody. They were both in love with each other, but she had allowed her head to control her endocrine emotions, and he still had heart emotions. They got together and found the mutual attraction was still there. She was now engaged, and he asked her to break it and marry him. After those many years of no contact, she still definitely made Hawkeye's hormones hum. The next day, she told the Colonel the situation and asked for an immediate transfer, which he granted. The two actors really played their parts extremely well. They came across to the audience as living a real situation, which they could not have done if there had not been some Androgynic Factor there in reality. Otherwise, you just can't fake it that well. The only problem in this show was that gynics (the real actor, Alan Alda) make the emotion-free decisions, but in this story it was the andric girlfriend who made it. The equal and opposite was cast there, and the characters played an excellent "natural" role of what hormones can do to people.

Back in the 1930's, Edward the 8th abdicated the throne of England to marry a woman who had been divorced. Horrors! Divorce was a big enough sin at that time to prevent him from continuing as the King of England if he married her. He stated that his love for this woman was stronger than his desire to be King. My hormone mentor, Dr. Melvin Page, would probably have titled the newspaper article covering the abdication as, "Throne Thrown for Hormone." Simple.

Simple to Dr. Melvin Page, who introduced me to a concept that I use many times every day. On the telephone, in personal interaction – even evaluating who will buy something advertised on TV and who will switch channels to avoid watching the ad.

How did I find out this information? By trying to find out where dental decay and gum disease came from. There is a connection? Actually, yes, there is a very big interconnection between health, disease, dentistry, marriage and business. Yeah, took me a while to sort all of that out, too.

How did I fall off the log of conventional drillum, fillum and billum dentistry? Was I looking for a marriage between diet and dentistry? Looking for biodentistry? Hardly. I was a frustrated tooth mechanic.

In 1968 I was very frustrated. I had taken postgraduate courses every month for 6 years and still did not feel that I had the basics of the subject of dentistry. Something was missing. I was looking again for that "something" while in the front row listening to Dr. Arne Lauritzen, who, with his distinctly Danish accent, was opening a door I knew I wanted to enter. This was the first day of a 5 day seminar. At the 10:30 a.m. break I approached the Great Dane and said:

"Dr. Lauritzen, I am going to leave now."

"Vhy?" he asked.

"Because I have already gotten my money's worth and don't want to cheat you."

I meant it. He had introduced me to the basic concepts of dentistry that I knew were the ones I had been seeking but had not been able to find in dental school or in those past 6 years of post-graduate courses. I had found the "source", if only I could digest and assimilate it.

After my second time through the same 5 day course, I knew there was far too much here for me to absorb. I asked Lauritzen if he had written a book on his techniques.

"Oh, no, no time for that. Besides I'm not very good at taking the time to write."

"I am a decent writer," I opened the conversation, not knowing why. I just knew that he had something I needed. I figured a good way to learn what this *fountain of proof* had to offer was to be his ghost writer. He had in his mind what all young dentists needed if they were to be able to do even the basics with confidence and accuracy. He knew how to make crowns and bridges that fit and that knew how to chew. He knew how to make dentures that would not fall out when the patient bit into corn on the cob. He knew all kinds of things that worked in daily practice – if you knew how to do the basics with accuracy. He turned my frustration into fascination.

"Let me tape record you, write up your techniques, have you correct my writings, and in no time you will have a book that all of us need."

That conversation led to a 5 year commitment of writing and rewriting his textbook, <u>Atlas of Occlusal Analysis</u>. The old buzzard was just as picky about words as he was about dental procedures. It took 8 rewrites before he was satisfied that the textbook contained the precision he wanted to present. I was pretty surprised at his superb knowledge of English. After all, English was his 4th language! He could lecture fluently in 6 languages, correct an interpreter in 3 more, and swear in 3 more.

During the second month of writing, he gave me an assignment that changed my life forever. An exciting change. This change led directly and unknowingly into the sea of interacting hormones that govern all of our daily personal interactions. I would be able to understand people. Even some women.

Lauritzen told me:

"All of this dentistry that we do with superb mechanical contrivances is doomed to failure if the mouth into which it is placed is not biologically sound. You are going to write the first chapter. It will be on the importance of nutrition. The patient must have sound nutrition in order for the body to regenerate itself. The people who come to see dentists with a mouth in disaster are also experiencing the same disaster in their whole body. The mouth is but the barometer of the total body's health."

"Barometers? Nutrition?" I queried. "I don't know the first thing about nutrition. We had one 50 minute class session in dental school in which we were told to refer people with diabetes to nutritionists. I want to learn about the hinge axis, centric relation, the use of the split cast and cusp fossa relationships. What does nutrition have to do with anything?"

Be careful for what you ask. You might get it.

I got answers to those questions. Oh, yes, I learned about hinge axis and other things a tooth mechanic needs to know, but after my 5 year "internship" with Lauritzen and his friends, I learned what it was to be a doctor of the oral cavity.

> *Be careful for what you ask. – You might get it!*

Lauritzen continued: "Here are the names and private telephone numbers of Dr. Melvin Page and Dr. Emanuel Cheraskin. Get their books, go see them personally, become educated in how to write that first chapter. It is the most important." Those were my marching orders. A piece of paper with two telephone numbers on it.

By the time I re-wrote that nutrition chapter well enough to please him, I was booked a year and a half in advance on the lecture circuit of dentistry. I was demonstrating how blood chemistry could be used to direct diets so that people no longer had dental decay or gum disease. That was fun. I liked being a ham in front of the bright lights while bringing a unique message. After all, by the time I was lecturing, I knew that Dr. Page had stopped rampant dental decay in its tracks for as long as 30 and 40 years. He had shown me the records. Hundreds of them. Why shouldn't we do the same thing? Better than fluoride.

My first visit to see Dr. Page on a Monday morning was not what I had anticipated. I found him with a tape in his hand, measuring forearms and calves and drawing lines on a strange looking graph. I thought I was going to see people drawing blood and analyzing it. They actually were – just in another room.

The laboratory. I noticed that they tested stool samples in there, too.

There was a great deal of intensity around these measuring procedures while he simultaneously mumbled instructions in some strange language to his assistant. She would motion for the patients to follow her, and they would disappear into another undisclosed inner sanctum of the office.

"Where are they going?" I queried.

"To the beach until Wednesday when I'll look at a new blood to see if the posterior pituitary worked," Page answered.

Oh, yeah. I thought that might be the case. What a bizarre world here at St. Petersburg Beach.

I went to the beach and rented a sail boat.

The next morning, Page had more time to spend with me and began to explain what was going on.

"You see, the problem is that modern technology, especially in the food industry, does not always think in terms of what is in the best interest for the health of the humans it is serving. The struggle for adaptation is going on, and – all about us – is seen the pitiful evidence of a losing fight.

"But, diet can't do everything. Some people expect too much from diet. *There are those who eat well, but are not well.* The effect of diet is limited by the mechanism of utilization of the foods eaten. Utilization of food is dependent upon breakdown and assimilation, which is controlled by the endocrine glands. Herein lies one of the secrets of health. Diet plus assimilation must be assured. Your endocrine glands are in charge of that. Assimilation and absorption are required for maintenance and reconstruction.

"Ever heard of the Hunzas?" he asked.

I could tell that this was going to be another avenue of investigation over which I had no control.

"No."

"Sir Robert McCarrison, a British physician, spent 7 years in India at a mountainous place called Hunza. There was no cancer. People lived to be 110 and died with all their own teeth. His conclusion was that this happens because of 3 simple factors absent in our lifestyle. They eat natural food, unrefined, grown on fertile soil, and they eat it fresh. In addition to that, they do not have endocrine glands disturbed by our modern way of life. It is obvious in today's professions that we ignore these aspects and practice *professional myopia*.

"Today, civilized man considers diet first if his animals are ill, drugs if his children are ill." That summed up a lot of Page's philosophy in a nutshell.

> *Today, civilized man considers diet first if his animals are ill, drugs if his children are ill.*

Page continued, "I was a member of the D.C. Jarvis Study Club for over 40 years. It was a group of 60 physicians and 2 dentists who were in a correspondence study club. Most of us never met each other face to face, but we knew each other's innermost thoughts. The study club went from about 1910 until 1955. These fellows were bright and innovative. Everyone who got a new idea of how to treat a disease would send their results to Jarvis, and he would think it through, then mimeograph the information and mail it to the rest of us. Others would pick up on the technique, modify and improve it, send it to Jarvis for comments, then the modifications and comments were mailed out again."

(As an aside, Page was the transcribing secretary for this club for 4 decades. Once he allowed me to photocopy about 15,000 pages of the Jarvis Group correspondence. That was a peek into historic conversations from a time without "miracle" drugs, and physicians had to be "real doctors". Some day I may write a brief synopsis of their methods. Without drugs, their primary treatment was to build up their patient's resistance to disease.)

Back to Page: "That was in the days when the best doctors were the ones who could find out how to build up the natural resistance of the body. Not like those today who try to find a drug to cover up symptoms so the patient will stop complaining and accept their lot."

Page seemed rather bitter as he said those last words.

"Was that the Dr. Jarvis of apple cider and vinegar for allergies fame?" I asked.

"Humph," Page replied. "That was probably the most highly insignificant piece of work Jarvis did, but it is the most popular. He was brilliant beyond any of us, and some of us were pretty smart. The Jarvis Group is where the idea of using small doses of hormones to stimulate the endocrine system came from. I liked the idea. I started using it in dentistry. It didn't take long to find that people with lots of dental decay had imbalances in thyroid activity. I would give small doses of thyroid – like a tenth or fiftieth of a grain to people, and some improved while others got worse.

"Looking at blood chemistries, I noticed that people with lots of dental decay had serum phosphorus levels that were below 3.5 milligrams percent, and those with little or no decay had phosphorus levels above 3.5, and at 4.0 milligrams, they had excellent oral health. Those people with 3.5 to 4.0 milligrams of phosphorus also had excellent physical and mental health. I started recommending that those people with low serum phosphorus levels take phosphorus supplements and eat foods rich in phosphorus – and nothing happened. Then I prescribed low doses of thyroid, and within 3 days, the serum phosphorus levels had started moving. Some the right direction, some wrong.

> *Looking at blood chemistries, I noticed that people with lots of dental decay had serum phosphorus levels that were below 3.5 mg%.*
> Dr. Melvin Page

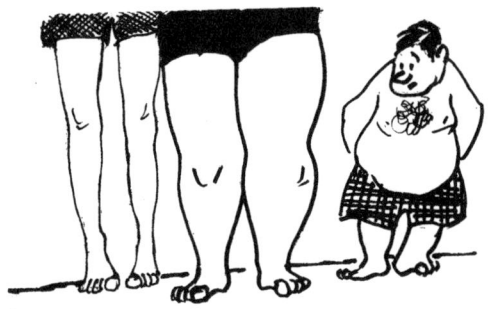

"Then I began to notice ankles."

"Ankles?"

"Yes. Those people with what I call thick ankles got better when I gave them thyroid, and those with thin ankles got worse. I could see this in how they looked and acted, but also in their blood chemistry changes. Thick ankled people needed thyroid stimulation, and thyroid supplements improved them both physically and chemically. Thin ankled people were probably hyper-thyroid to begin with, and added hormone just make them worse. It was all in their blueprint. It was genetically preordained.

> *Thick ankled people needed thyroid stimulation.*

"Took about 10 years of observing these findings until I developed the graph that I use today. It's pretty accurate. Lot better than guessing endocrine function. People's bodies tell you a lot – if you just know where to look."

Micro endocrinology was the term Page used to describe his method of using small doses of the actual hormone to jump start stalled endocrine activity. It seemed to be similar in concept to homeopathy, except that the dosages were not that small. Not as large as conventional medicine used, however. He told me that the human body manufactured about three and a half grains of thyroid hormone per lifetime, and that some people took that much every day. High doses shut down the thyroid gland – something over one half grain – and you lived entirely on the pill.

"The body may make as many as 20 different thyroid hormone subsets, and medication thyroid probably doesn't contain these. By stimulating the body to manufacture its own hormone, you get what you need – specifically designed by your body just for you."

That made sense to me, but did it work, and how long did it take?

Sure enough, by Wednesday the woman Page had sent to the beach returned and the posterior pituitary supplement had altered the specific gravity of the urine and raised the serum phosphorus level. Two to three days. Not bad. As it turned out, all of the hormones produced significant changes within three days. Sometimes the changes were the right way, and sometimes not, but the majority were the right way.

"How do you know what hormone to use and how much to use?"

"The graph helps me. It tells the *original* blueprint of the body. I start with that. Some people have had endocrine surgery, an accident, or are on a medication that interferes with normal hormonal production. That is when I need a blood test to tell me whether I am over-dosing, under-dosing, or am right on target."

"How does the graph tell you this? What is this graph thing anyway?"

Page showed me a complex box with little boxes at both sides. Lots of mathematics seemed to take place on both sides of the original graph. It meant nothing more to me than it would to you. Eventually, I learned that all of our hormones have counterparts, and when the parts and counterparts lined up, equal and opposite, someone was going to make your hormones hum.

To simplify the measurement concept, I shall show only the central core of the graph:

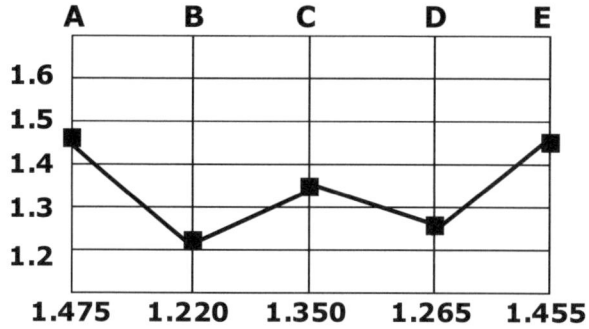

Page continued:

"Deposition of muscle and fat are under endocrine influence. So is bone growth. All of this is determined at the moment of conception. Hormones guide bone growth for length and thickness; then hormones direct the deposition of muscle and fat onto those bones. The result is what we look like.

"Malfunction of the glandular system can be detected by observing the effect on the configuration of the person. (Their body shape.) Over-activity or under-activity of any one of the glands will result in either the accumulation or loss of tissue in specific parts of the body. You just have to know where to look. It's all right in front of you, literally. Learn to look, and while you are at it, learn to observe.

> *Malfunction of the glandular system can be detected by observing the effect on the configuration of the person.*

"Body, or anthropometric measurements as they are called, in addition to a series of exacting blood tests, are the tools of my approach to controlling degenerative diseases. Measurements of body lengths and circumferences make a retrograde evaluation of underlying systemic invitations to disease onset – if that person is in the presence of external challenges. This recognition of the fundamental importance of body shape as an indicator of disease susceptibility is essential in my approach to the control of degenerative disease. It could serve as a starting point in modern research for the study of the causes and prevention of predictable degenerative processes."

Four decades after hearing that, I can now understand the insightful significance of that statement. Yes, even today, research would be far advanced if it paid homage to Page's observations. But, as I remember instructions from one professor during my years working on my post doc master's, "Do not use references that are more than two years old, for they are too old to be of any significance today." My andric spirit at that time caused me to retort, "Does that mean that the Bible is of no significance?" Didn't get me any extra credit points, but immediately established me as a non-conforming rebel in the eyes of that professor.

Page continued:

"Basically, the body is divided into two halves at the navel. The upper torso develops under the influence of one set of endocrine glands, while the lower half develops under the influence of its counter hormones."

> The body is divided into two halves at the navel.

"I never heard of a counter hormone. What in the world is that?"

"You have heard of equal and opposite, haven't you? Like protons being balanced by electrons in the nucleus? There is exactly the same amount of positive charge in a proton as there is equal and opposite negative charge in each electron in the outer shells. Lose an electron, and you just created an electrochemical reaction. You can measure the influence of saturated outer shell electrons versus those that are missing an electron. This imbalance may create affirmative chemical action, or inhibitory, depending on which element is involved."

I was beginning to get the same feeling about blood chemistry as I had about Lauritzen and his evaluations of jaw function. There was apt to be more to this than eating a piece of fish to balance the blood chemistry.

"So what are the hormone equal and opposites? Is this like matter and antimatter?"

"Nothing so complex."

I was glad to hear that. I had already suffered enough complexity since meeting Lauritzen and was ready to grasp something simple.

"Endocrine action is designed in pairs. Each endocrine gland has its counter part, or, in some cases, counter parts. There may be two glands working in opposition to one, but, generally, it is one to one. About that lady I gave posterior pituitary to on Monday—she should have balanced with estrogen alone, but didn't. She didn't require any more estrogen, but wasn't balancing; so I added a second counterpart that would potentiate the estrogen without overstimulating the estrogen manufacturing system. That was the purpose of using posterior pituitary hormone. Should have known that by looking at her hips. She has a double dip hip, so posterior pituitary should help her relationship with her husband – as well as with everyone else – and give me the chemistry I am looking for."

I was happy for this "non-complex" answer. God sometimes puts me into uncharted, choppy waters, but frequently forgets to give me a compass. In those cases, my only choice is to listen.

"When endocrine pairs are working 50-50 with each other, things are in balance. I can see this by watching the serum phosphorus level. When the phosphorus is 4.0 milligrams

> *When endocrine pairs are working 50-50 with each other, things are in balance.*

percent, each gland of the pair is carrying 50% of the load – sort of, for they are opposites at the same time. If one is overstimulated, resulting in a 60-40 relationship, then the phosphorus level will be less than 4.0. This is OK down to 3.6 milligrams, but when it drops below 3.5 we have dropped from a *regeneration* phase to a *degeneration* phase. We have moved from wellness to sickness."

"What's this about the relationship between her and her husband?" I asked, since this was about the only thing I got from the conversation.

"Body language told me that their relationship was not too comfortable. It was OK when they got married, but it has changed, and he is not sure what has happened."

"Look," I said, "I was in on that case the whole time with you. There was no conversation remotely related to their compatibility. In fact, he said very little during the whole appointment."

Page retorted, "Typical of gynic males. They will sit back and let their andric wives do all the talking, unless something really oblique comes up. You see, the posterior pituitary is one of the primary 'I'm OK, you're OK' glands. When you eat as much sugar and coffee as she does, glandular secretions are reduced and her interpretation of humanity is that no one is OK. Her double dip hip tells me that even small amounts of coffee or sugar will impact her posterior pituitary. You can see that real evidently on the graph, too. Coffee and sugar can cause disharmony in relationships with anyone she talks to."

"I noticed that she had a tendency to be testy toward you."

"That's another matter. She is andric, and I am andric. We will never be able to discuss controversial topics without a spat. That is why I just told her what to do and did not launch into lengthy explanations. She would pick me apart – not listen to what I am trying to do to help her – and we would not have a good chemistry or successful case. Her husband's graph is equal and opposite to hers, and that is why he stays around but is confused about what happened to the woman he married."

"You didn't do his graph," I blurted out, trying not to be offensive, but trying to keep the conversation somewhat on track. I was there. I watched him graph her, but he hardly more than glanced at the husband, much less took the time to run all these measurements.

Page looked at me and grinned. "You are going to fall head over heels in love with chemistry," he said. "You're the curious type, and chemistry never loses its mystique. You will always be searching for yet another answer. Watch me graph the husband. I will show you the equal and opposite lines, and then let you worry about how I knew the answer before measuring. The truth is, I already looked. I can see the blueprint of his endocrines by looking at his body form. Especially with him wearing a T-shirt, short pants and sandals. Believe me, I know. You are an andric," he said looking at me.

"Actually, I'm an Aries."

He ignored the comment and continued, "I've seen over 50,000 chemistries and still get fascinated with each new one I see. You will do the same."

At the time, I did not share his enthusiasm. I was here on assignment to learn about nutrition. Chemistry was not my best subject in college. Chemistry and I were equal and opposite.

Page was right, though. When I learned to speak the language of human blood chemistry, I found a whole new world totally different from the smelly college chemistry laboratory.

Blood chemistry was as alive as the person it came from. The best part was that I could show patients how to control their own chemical destiny. I learned how to generate enthusiasm in patients by letting them know that they were in control of their own health. They did not have to be 'drug dependent' upon multiple bottles of prescription medications designed to cover symptoms. I, too, became enchanted with the mystique.

Even after 35 years of watching (up 'til now, 34,000 chemistries), just like Page, I am still fascinated.

By the way, Page did do the husband's graph, and it <u>was</u> equal and opposite to his wife's. Mystique. I did write the nutrition chapter, and after multiple rewrites, Lauritzen accepted it. Miracle.

Before bidding me farewell to attack the seas with a rented sailboat, Page left me with another thought provoking commentary about a question I had asked him earlier. Evidently he had been thinking about the question, "What about those genetically imbalanced people? Are they doomed to a life of disease?"

Page answered, "A person's endocrine pattern is an important factor in his qualities of mind, personality and aptitude. Those born with endocrine patterns diverging from the normal are often valuable contributors to society. Their skills and abilities may be of highly unusual quality. Olympic contenders in any field, so to speak. The endocrine pattern which produces these favorable factors unfortunately may simultaneously produce liabilities from the pathological point of view. They may have a shorter life span than the average. They tend to overdo and burn out early.

> *A person's endocrine pattern is an important factor in his qualities of mind, personality and aptitude.*

"Balancing these people's chemistries does not change their basic personality, but it can remove the barriers to their <u>real</u> personality. This can create a problem if the person was rather dull and in a dull satisfactory marriage. If one mate becomes more bright and productive, it

> *Balancing these people's chemistries does not change their basic personality, but it can remove the barriers to their <u>real</u> personality.*

may challenge an insecure mate and disturb the relationship. You must learn that the human body cannot be divided into compartments and create isolated treatments directed toward one compartment. You cannot treat a tooth and ignore the systemic, physical and emotional parts of that person. The whole must be considered in designing treatment."

Another interesting observation / prediction from Page that I have seen prove to be true is: "With the advent of antibiotics, I saw a victory over the common infectious diseases, but simultaneously there was a steadily rising mortality from degenerative diseases. Most of this new mortality takes its toll in the prime period of these people's lives, and often from the most valuable contributors to our society."

Thoughts for another time.

The Hormone Fascination

Now I'll focus on the other fascination that grew out of my ten years of education with Dr. Page. How Hormones Hum.

I shall try to assemble my disjointed education about something practically no one has ever heard about into a more cohesive package. It took a few years and watching thousands of people inter-reactions before I got the grasp I feel now. Opposite endocrine patterns were the key. Historically, many people had mentioned the concept of "opposites attract". I remember my Mother's observation on this concept when I mentioned it to her.

"With teens – just being male and female is opposite enough," she said.

Close, but that does not offer much for long term relationships.

Page used to instruct his secretary to bring people into his office slowly, by perhaps pointing out the view, a bronze, a picture, the furniture, anything to make them turn right and left so he could see them from a side, front and back view before actually being introduced to them. I asked him about this, and he explained that he was visually checking out their blue-prints before evaluating them. Saved a lot of time, because this pre-flight check told him how to talk to the patient.

"If an architect draws a plan, a builder can build a building. If the same architect sees a building that is already built, he could probably draw the blueprints by measuring the building. Right?"

"I'm with you so far," I stated cautiously.

"DNA is your blueprint. Your body is built according to that. But after the person is an adult, you can take measurements of the body and retro-draw the blueprint. Remember, the deposition of muscle and fat, as well as the growth of bones, is under endocrine influence.

"There is a point of perfect functional balance between these paired endocrine glands. When this is present, the patient has maximum resistance to attack from disease-producing conditions.

"The goal of Mother Nature is to have everybody in that perfect balance of disease resistance. At that point, you will also be able to interact with other humans in a positive manner – devoid of unproductive battles. Pretty decent goal and purpose, wouldn't you say? Well, the way to achieve that utopia is to have people with opposite endocrine patterns mate. Their progeny will be not quite as hyper-active as the one parent, and not quite as hypo-functional as the other. They will have a better blueprint for survival.

> *The goal of Mother Nature is to have everybody in that perfect balance of disease resistance.*

"When a male is near a female with the opposite endocrine patterns, he is attracted to her, and she to him. This attraction can be modified to a slight degree depending on the social mores in which they were raised, but the feelings will still be there.

"This attraction is present even if the people do not speak the same language, are not the same age, not the same race or don't have the same social graces.

"Extreme hypers are attracted to extreme hypos, but, although they do not understand their mate's responses to situations, they somehow work things out and stay together. The closer to the perfect balance point a person is, the more attracted he/she is to a mate who is also close to the balance point, and they will have the more externally apparent harmonious life together.

"Endocrine 'likes' can like each other, and even work together on short term projects where there is a definitive external goal. But! As marriage partners, beware. It will not last. Sometimes people meet in Las Vegas, have a wonderful fling and get married the same week. Then, as time etches their emotional surfaces, friction develops. They become angry with each other over small matters – misunderstand the 'meaning' of what they say to each other – and, in short, divorce is in their future.

"That's OK. Let them separate. If people of the same endocrine patterns are forced to stay together, one will hurt – even kill – the other, in order to get out of the situation. In some cases where social or religious pressure forces them to stay together, one may develop an incurable disease and die in order to get out of the situation. Why? Because Mother Nature knows that if two people of similar endocrine pattern mate and produce a child, the child will be more apt to have birth defects, have low resistance to disease and in short, experience an unpleasant life. This is not in accord with Mother Nature's plan for peace, good will and survival on Planet Earth.

"If a hyperthyroid and a hyperthyroid produce a child, the child will be double plus hyperthyroid which leads to hyper-hyper susceptibility to disease. The same is true for all of the endocrine pairs. But, there is a natural protection against birth defects in these cases. Many times two people of similar endocrine patterns will not even talk to each other for more than a few seconds. They may take offense to each other within the first ten seconds of mis-interpreted sentences they exchange. There are negative 'vibes' that enhance this meeting. Excellent form of birth control. More on this later."

Pre-Marriage Predictions

Page secretly wanted to be a pre-marriage counselor. He felt that in 15 minutes he could accurately determine a couple's chances of establishing a mutually satisfying long term relationship. He was probably right, but his sometimes brusque way of presenting the results might not have gained him many referrals. His manner of presentation might be something like this: "Yep. You are good for each other," or "Nope, won't work. You are not matched. Each of you find someone else." I saw him do that to a young newly-engaged couple. I still remember the facial looks of horror that came over each of them as they stood in front of Page, affectionately holding hands. I remember the frozen expression and chill I experienced when I measured my fiancée. I only measured one side, because I didn't want to know any more. If Page was right, this marriage was doomed. But I was really in love. This was different. It superceded the graph concept. Page was wrong. I could not be dissuaded. I never told her the truth about the results. Twenty years after our divorce, she still has cutting things to say about me.

> *The purpose of male and female living together is to produce a family that is better able to resist the attacks of living on Earth than their parents.*

To reiterate. The purpose of male and female living together is to produce a family that is better able to resist the attacks of living on Earth than their parents. To build resistance. Tolerance. Understanding of their fellow man. The world is full of changes in temperature, bacteria, viruses, natural disasters, and emotional conflict among ourselves. All of these things produce stress. Stress compromises our immune system and allows some of us to catch the flu, diabetes, cancer, have a heart attack, or in some way succumb to the rigors challenging our existence. Some catch these diseases early in life and die from not being able to overcome the challenge, while others may live (as Page did) well into their 90's. What's the difference?

The difference is *internal resistance*. The ability to cope. We can do some things to increase or reduce our ability to resist challenge. These things were logical 100 years ago, but have been modified by advertising in today's world. Which would increase or decrease your ability to resist disease? A high protein diet, vegetarian diet, drinking lots of milk, vegetating in front of a TV set, drinking a glass of wine daily, a bottle of wine daily, working a 4 day week, 6 day week, wearing dark glasses outside, taking prescription drugs, elicit drugs, taking calcium or vitamin B-12, eating everything from cans, eating nothing from cans, eating chocolate, taking early retirement, wearing clothes made from artificial fibers, having a big family??? Before studying body chemistry, I would have missed over half of these questions. By using endocrine patterns as part of our lifestyle evaluation process, we can find that we are not all alike. We do not respond the same way to challenges. Sometimes that is nice to know.

We cannot change our innate resistance. That's up to our hormones. But! We can modify our internal reactions to external challenges by living lifestyles that increase our protection against our deficiencies and reduce our overactive endocrines. We are what we are. Surgical intervention can create some differences, but the original *pattern* is still there.

Picking up on thyroid again, let's look at it from the physical and biological standpoint, then the emotional. *Physically*, the hyperthyroid person will run a higher cholesterol, have a decreased phosphorus level making that person more susceptible to early degeneration and slow recovery from physical challenges. Hyperthyroid people show more abnormal reactivity to challenges that lead to reduction of resistance and the onset of disease more easily. The boat overturns in chilly water. Most people swim to safety; one dies of a heart attack in the water. Why? Inability to cope with the challenge.

You could almost say the same things about the hypothyroid person. Only he will have a low cholesterol, also a decreased phosphorus leading to lack of resistance to challenge, will have slow recovery to physical challenges, and may also die in the boating accident because he cannot pull up the extra effort to swim to shore.

Another overturned boat – this time farther from shore. Everyone starts swimming for shore. The water is cold and two people make it to shore. The rest die in the attempt. One of the survivors is discharged from the hospital the next morning, the other contracts pneumonia and dies a few days later. The two who survived had superior endocrine patterns, but one had a perfect balance between thyroid and pancreas, while the other had only a near-perfect balance. That is the purpose of life. Perhaps it is a modification of survival of the fittest. If it works, we will eventually develop a race of humans that have perfect balances between all of their endocrine glands. This would produce a race with maximum resistance to disease, to challenges, and – be very stable emotionally.

From the *emotional* standpoint, let's examine the extremes. The very hyperthyroid versus the very hypothyroid. (Most of us are somewhere in between. These stories are exemplary of the polar ends of endocrinology.)

A pencil rolls off the table onto the floor. The hyperthyroid wife yells, "Pick up that pencil, quick!" Her hypothyroid husband slowly drops his chin to look over his glasses at the situation.

"It's just a pencil. I'll get it when I go to the 'fridge to get a beer." He obviously underestimates the severity of the situation, so his hyperthyroid wife feels *obligated* to take a few moments to educate him about his deficient evaluation.

"Someone might come in here, slip on that pencil, fall and break something, go to the hospital, then sue us for everything we have, and we won't be able to send the kids to college, so they will be undereducated and poor and end up living with us the rest of their lives, and we'll have to take care of their kids."

"Awww, you're overreacting again. As usual."

"You just don't understand the significance of what can happen. You never worry about the future."

This is typical of two polar opposite endocrine controlled people who do not view the identical situation in any similar fashion. They are polar opposites in both interpretation and solution. Yet they stay together – for 50 years – and continue to bicker about the difference between major and minor events. But! They do not get upset with each other. It may look like a full scale war to the outsider, but it is just discussion to them.

> *They are polar opposites in both interpretation and solution —yet they stay together.*

What about people who are close to that perfect line of balance? They are attracted to someone of the opposite sex who is <u>also</u> close to the line. They can really have a nice comfortable life together. They are the ones who call themselves "soul mates". The rest of us? We represent the majority. We have our ups and downs, but somehow seem to be able to work things out. In these personal relationships, solutions are more important than winning or losing – for the most part. This may require some degree of kiss and make up, but that only happens if the endocrine patterns are compatible. Equal and opposite. You really do want to be close to that person. You miss them when they are away.

Graphic Examples

So what about the graphs? What magic do they hold? How do you interpret them? Perhaps first, we should figure out how to graph a person. As with anything, there has to be a starting point. The starting point is the estrogen - testosterone balance. The Androgynic Factor. A reasonably accurate measurement is found from bony measurements: the length of the lower arm versus the length of the leg; and by measuring the wrist and ankle. There are specific points to measure, but the overview looks like this.

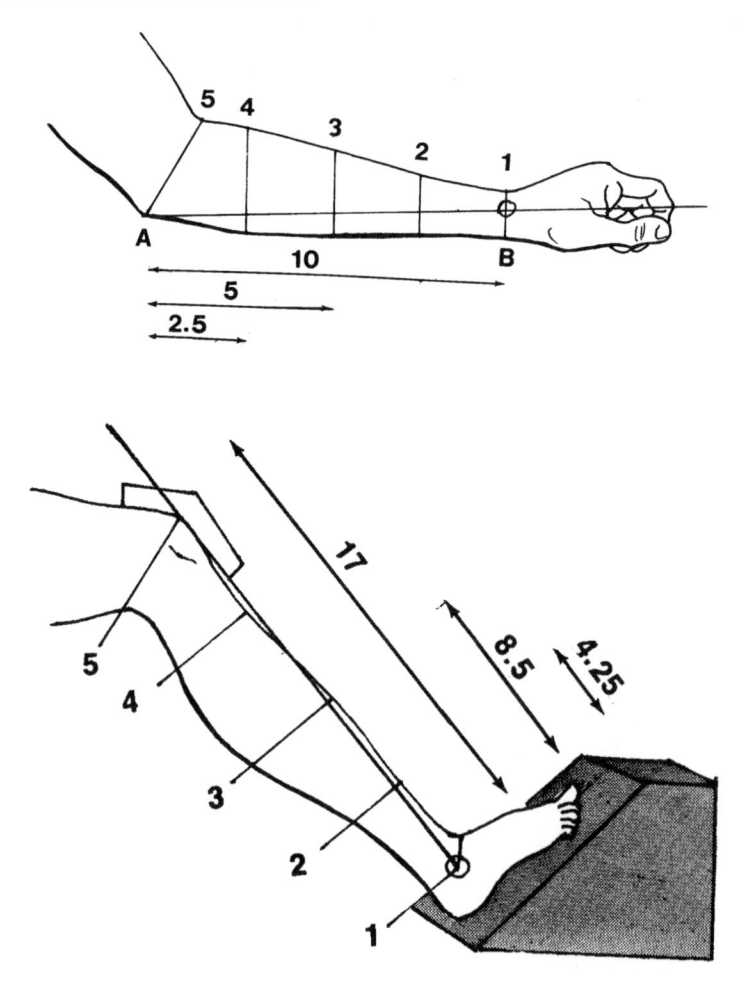

The forearm measurement is divided into the leg measurement to obtain a number that is the "starting point" of the graph.

This point is registered on the "A" column of the graph. There is a letter "F" on the "A" column that represents the ideal starting point for females and a letter "M" on another graph as the reference point for males. For males the ideal starting point is 1.475, and for females it is 1.550. If the client is lower than these figures, the client is *gynic* (or estrogen dominant); if the figure is higher than the ideal, the client is *andric* (or testosterone dominant).

Optimum FEMALE Graph

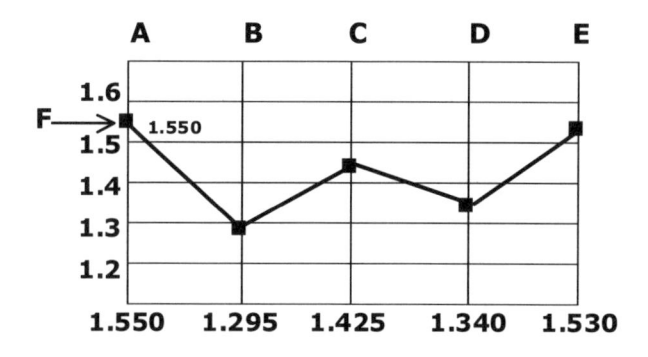

	A	B	C	D	E
	1.550	1.295	1.425	1.340	1.530

F → 1.550

Optimum MALE Graph

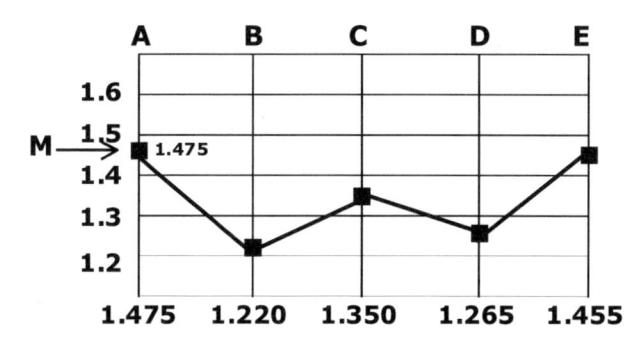

	A	B	C	D	E
	1.475	1.220	1.350	1.265	1.455

M → 1.475

Let's start with our hypo-hyper couple of a few pages ago. Physically, we know that the hyperthyroid is easy to spot because of thin ankles. This is the intense partner. The hypothyroid has thicker ankles, and they are the laid back partner. Another item you may see on occasion is that you will find little beads of perspiration on the upper lip of the hypothyroid person when even the slightest stress is present. They are constantly wiping their upper lip.

But, by measuring the wrist and ankle according to the following directions, and dividing the wrist measurement into the ankle measurement, you will come up with a number. That number corresponds to a place on the graph.

Note the "B" column, second from the left. This represents the action between thyroid and the pancreas (which produces insulin). The graph is labeled *hypo thyroid* and *hyper thyroid*, because that is the interpretation used most often for treatment selection. Page treated hypothyroid conditions with small dosages of thyroid hormone (one tenth to one hundredth of a grain), and hyperthyroid conditions with 3 units of insulin.

Now look at the blow up figure of that part specifically:

Hypo / Hyper Thyroid

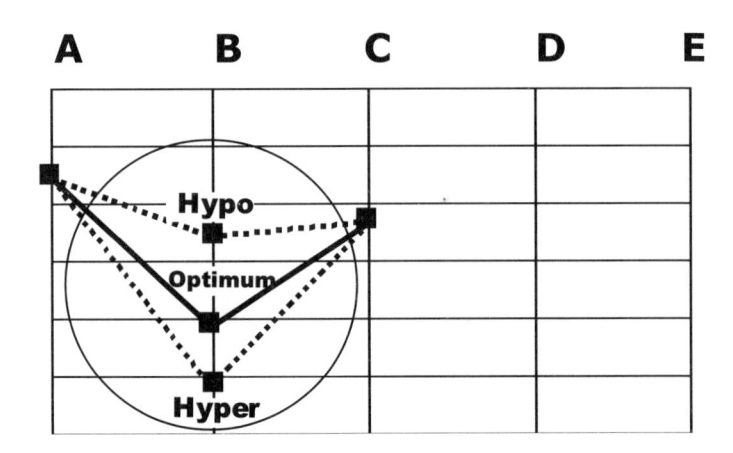

The measurements give you a number on the vertical axis that can be plotted just above or below the point of the "V" on the "B" line.

The solid line represents the ideal reference line. The upper dashed line indicates a hypo thyroid condition. The dashed line that is below the solid line represents a hyper thyroid endocrine blueprint. If this represented two different people, one male, the other female, these folks would be just about equal and opposite – certainly close enough to get along as far as thyroid function is concerned. This is only *part* of the story, however.

Our primary goal is to determine the balance of activity in what is called the autonomic nervous system. It is the automatic pilot of all the involuntary processes such as respiration, heart rate, digestion, elimination and body temperature just to cover some basics. It is divided into two sections, not surprisingly – equal and opposite. They are called the sympathetic and a parasympathetic divisions.

Sympathetic = Rush ahead
Parasympathetic = slow down

Mouthfull. Interpretation: They are the *rush ahead* and the *slow down* glands. In the *sympathetic* division (rush ahead) – a familiar example is adrenalin (but thyroid is similar). This creates the fight response. The go forward response. This is also known as the tear down response. When your engine is going at its maximum speed, it is wearing out faster. When you have a disease, the sympathetic division is overworking. It is still spinning its wheels – wearing out the tires – and getting nowhere.

Counter to the sympathetic division is the *parasympathetic* division of the autonomic nervous system. This is the calm down and repair division. During the treatment of disease, our goal is to slow down the destructive action of the sympathetic division, and increase the reconstructive activity of the parasympathetic division.

From the standpoint of the endocrine pattern, the hyperthyroid patient will be more difficult to heal than the hypothyroid, because you have to tame the wild beast (sympathetic division) before parasympathetic controlled healing can take place. This you can tell by a glance at the graph. If the patient's graph line is <u>below</u> the ideal line, the patient is hyper-thyroid.

As far as thyroid's action is concerned, it is similar to the short stop in baseball. He doesn't cover any particular base – doesn't protect the team from a home run from the opposition very often, but for any infield play, he can become very important for short periods of time. Thyroid helps scope out the person of the opposite sex, but doesn't make any of the major advance or retreat decisions.

The next *up* spike in the graph (column "C") represents the <u>posterior pituitary gland</u>. This gland is highly protected by the skull. It is fairly near the center of the head. It, together with your thyroid gland, controls your emotions. From the medical standpoint, the posterior pituitary gland controls the kidney's

Hypo / Hyper Posterior Pituitary

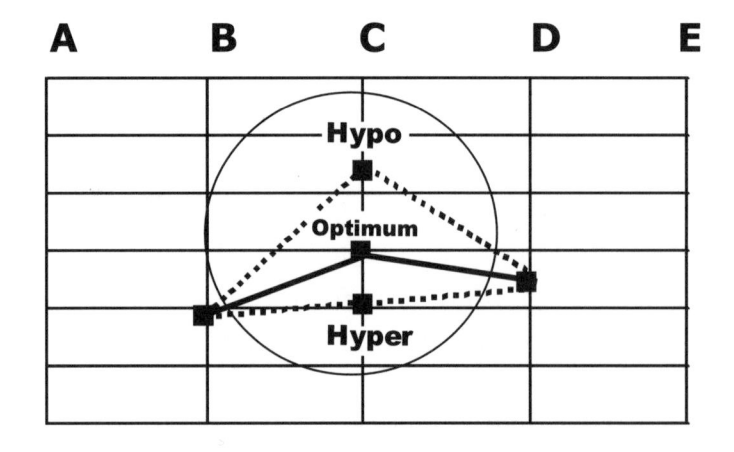

ability to concentrate urine. For this reason, testing what is called the specific gravity of the urine, or weight of a specific amount of urine relative to pure water, gives a confirmation of how well that gland is performing at the present time.

The posterior pituitary gland is very sensitive to the presence of sugar. As sugar enters the diet, urinary specific gravity goes down because posterior pituitary production of hormones is dropping. There goes your I'm OK, you're OK hormone. At a specific gravity of 1.022, all is quite well with the world. At 1.018, things are OK, but iffy. By 1.010, life with you is a juggling act between depression and being reasonable. Never know what is going to set you off. Below 1.008 indicates definite depression. To top it off, drop to 1.003, and we are in the severe suicidal thought range. Can't tell where the thoughts are coming from, but they float in uninvited many times each day. Not that you would do it, but the disturbing thoughts are there. People who do commit suicide are apt to be in this range, however.

Sugar is not the only thing that can reduce posterior pituitary function. Caffeine and alcohol are heavy contributors to exacerbate the situation. Coffee, tea, any alcoholic beverages, and Ooops—I almost forgot—chocolate. It does the same thing, except that the thiobromine in chocolate is 23 times stronger than caffeine. Drat!

And what about the other part of my life? Dentistry. Is this influential? Mercury comes out of the silver-mercury fillings during eating, drinking acidic or hot beverages, and just sitting there experiencing their self generated electrical currents. From the mouth, mercury travels up into the nasal cavities. From here mercury has but a one-inch trip to make up through the roof of the mouth into the posterior pituitary gland. Do you suppose this explains dentists' bizarre behavior – especially when something is different from the standard no-brainer activities? Dentists are noted for overreacting to minor events. Ask a dental assistant or family member willing to disclose the innermost secrets. It's worse than covering up alcoholism. Dentists have held the dubious honor for several decades for being number one in suicide. What is the major side-effect of exposure to mercury vapor? Suicidal and other violent bizarre thoughts. Road rage? They don't even have to be driving. In autopsy studies done by Nylander in Stockholm, Sweden, dentists were found to have 60,000 times more mercury in their posterior glands than human beings. Suggestive of anything?

> *Do you suppose this explains dentists' bizarre behavior ...like over reacting to minor events?*

Not everyone responds to sugar, alcohol and caffeine the same way. Can you predict who will respond the most? Yes. Look at the body. A male who is hypo-post pit will have a bald spot at the crown of his head.

The female develops what Page called the "double dip hip". This is perhaps easier to spot if females are wearing a bathing suit or slacks. Women are conscious of this condition by age 3 according to Page. If you look at a female child striking a cheesecake pose, as she will when trying to convince Daddy to do something she wants – you know – the pose that shows that she is so cute Daddy cannot possibly say "no", she will subliminally re-contour the appearance of her double dip hip.

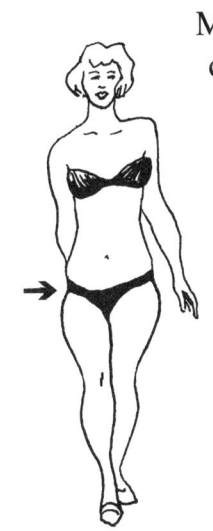

Mama still remembers how to compensate the double dip hip by striking a pose that over-emphasizes one hip to give it the more natural and appealing smooth curve. Must be genetic. Inborn in the species.

These folks, the 'hypo-post-pit' as Page called them, are most susceptible to emotional instability. Kids who are hypo-post pit don't have a chance. They see soft drinks advertisements targeted toward convincing kids that they can be 'athletically superior', or 'an accepted member of their society'. Soft drinks are cheap and easy to obtain. Usually they contain a pretty strong hit of both sugar and caffeine. Something like 8 tablespoons of sugar and 35 to 50 milligrams of caffeine per 8 ounce serving. But, who buys the 8 ounce can? Check out the grocery stores and see how many liter bottles are in the grocery carts.

I have seen biochemistry upsets and physical signs at as low a dosage as 8 milligrams of caffeine. Hypo-post-pit adults are more apt to indulge in coffee. Most coffees contain 120 or more milligrams of caffeine. Especially those that "really taste good". Taste? You are getting an alkaloid high. That has nothing to do with flavor.

Now, add to the equation the common dental silver-mercury amalgam filling with 35 micrograms of mercury being released per filling per day. Of course the 35 micrograms daily assumes that you do not disturb the filling by eating or drinking or chewing gum. These events further increase the mercury release factor. Each item does not mathematically *add* to body insult, because, in toxicity, the addition of one toxin plus another does not equal two. For instance, one unit of mercury and one unit of lead equals 60 times the toxic destruction of either individually. How can one determine the toxicity of sugar plus caffeine plus mercury? What if we include nickel from braces? Exponential.

> *A child's grade point average can be expected to drop 1½ points when they get braces.*

Teachers have told me that a child's grade point average can be expected to drop one and a half points when they get braces. They also see an immediate onset of "teenage behavior". Maybe this is not because they are "abnormal" by virtue of being teens, but that their hormone guidance system is malfunctioning due to toxicity.

How Does the Other Half Live?

<u>Thyroid</u> is the other half of I'm OK, You're OK, and it is affected by sugar, alcohol, caffeine, mercury and nickel as well. Any wonder that the number one cause of death in teens is suicide? Without thyroid and posterior pituitary hormones active, it is surprising to me that we have as stable a teen community as we have. If they all ran around killing each other, I could explain that. All of these biochemical and toxic insults accumulate during their *fetal development* and *childhood*, then express themselves at maximum velocity at about the age of the notable teen events at Columbine High School.

I got many letters and e-mails at the time following Columbine telling me that the senders had sent communications to police and others in Denver to check into this possible relationship. How many calls do you suppose I received from the many investigators? You got it. If there were anything wrong with sugar, alcohol, caffeine, mercury and nickel, surely the FDA, ADA, AMA, CIA – someone with three initials – would protect us.

Although not in common usage today, 50 years ago the Jarvis Group that Page mentioned earlier frequently used posterior pituitary extract to enhance emotional stability. I think a friend of mine expressed its abilities best. George called me on a Saturday a few years ago.

"You meet me at your office, pronto!"

"Sure, but why?"

"I need more of that pituitary stuff."

"But I'll be seeing you Monday morning. Why not give it to you at that time?"

"We've got a family reunion tomorrow and I ran out of the pills day before yesterday. I need it now, because when I take it, it changes the personality of the <u>next 200 people I meet</u>."

George knew that he would be tossing a few beers, eating desserts and doing other things that would unstabilize him, so he wanted his vibrant personality protected in the form of a pill.

Page had found that 88% of the women he measured were deficient in the genetic ability to produce adequate posterior pituitary hormones. (In males it was 56%.) That was higher than would be expected, so I quizzed him about it.

Page explained it this way: "Genetics can be passed along in the desired fashion of improving what you pass on relative to what you and your spouse can supply, but genetics can also be altered if you do not supply the proper raw materials. Or if you supply interference. If a female has a somewhat hypofunctioning posterior pituitary and is eating sugar, chocolate and caffeine during pregnancy, the development of that gland will not be in accordance with the genetic template. It may have been deficient, but will now be even more deficient. The template is there, it just does not get all of its dance card filled out at the right times."

I had never thought about that. I figured that genetics was a stable event. Two plus two equals four. Not so. Just because you have all the keys on a piano does not mean you will play a song without missing a note somewhere.

Anterior pituitary was another hormone that Page balanced,

Hypo / Hyper
Anterior Pituitary

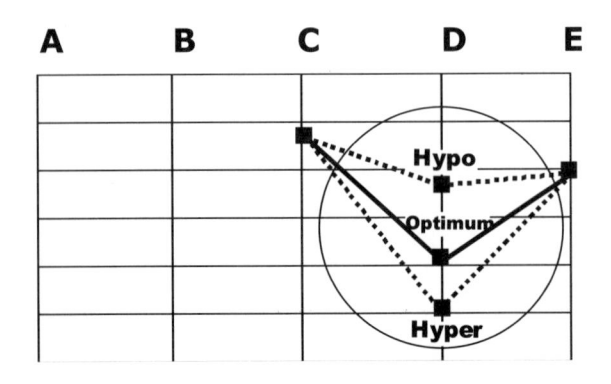

but I was never comfortable working with it. Overdose relative to what the patient needs, and you have just stimulated the body to think about forming cancer cells. Forget it. There was plenty to work with without walking that close to the edge.

Insulin cropped up again as a modifier (or counter hormone) to an overactive anterior pituitary gland just like in the case of an overactive thyroid gland. Page was able to use insulin as a deterrent to cancer growth, but I was happy to let him travel that road. There is too much grief given to folks who use alternative cancer therapy, especially if it is inexpensive.

I did, and still do, recommend the use of insulin. It actually has *many* attributes. I have a one hour lecture on the non-diabetic uses of insulin. It is great for post-surgical healing. In the oral cavity, one needs far less pain medication, and healing is so fast it is unbelievable. In my lectures I frequently state, "When injecting insulin, get the needle out fast, or it will heal in place." Maybe not quite that fast, but it makes its point. 3 units. "Too small a dose to be effective" is what most pharmacists or doctors will say, but Page's 40 years of using it and my additional 35 years have taught me what it can do.

> *One needs far less pain medication and healing is so fast it is unbelievable.*

From the endocrine balancing standpoint, insulin in small doses will slow down a hyper-functioning thyroid gland. So will taking radioactive iodine to kill thyroid cells, or surgically removing the thyroid gland. Using 3 units of insulin twice a week for a few weeks may accomplish the same thing without losing your thyroid gland for the rest of your life.

I now speak on the 55 non-diabetic uses of insulin. A specific type. Protamine Zinc Insulin (PZI). One that was removed from the market over the past few years and replaced with bacterially manufactured, genetically engineered insulin. Not my favorite. The original is still available in some foreign countries. It had many uses, and, at one time, I estimate that over 5000 physicians and dentists were using it on a routine basis. It is far cheaper than the drugs that were used to replace it, so perhaps that was a removal factor. Pain control, reduction of high blood pressure, elimination of shingles in 3 days, speeding healing of broken bones, lots of benefits gone by the wayside. I sound like an old man lamenting the good old days, don't I? Well, if the shoe fits...but I digress.

Insulin is one of the parasympathetic hormones. It heals. It calms. It is the equal and opposite to thyroid. Without injecting insulin, production of the hormone can be increased by having adequate protein in the diet. How much? Whatever it takes to keep your protein chemistries in the proper range. I think I've written about that in another book, but the overall problem of inadequate insulin seems to involve several things. Inadequate protein intake as a result of popular advertising, ingesting of drugs, taking excessive calcium supplements, and, in many cases, inadequate *digestion* of protein. My plan is not to eliminate protein, but to increase your body's ability to digest and metabolize it. After all, protein is what your body is made out of.

Don't forget that mercury from fillings can bind to the action sites of insulin. Mercury is a big fan of insulin binding sites and can play a big role in the creation of diabetes. Having insulin in place is one thing, but having it there and inactivated by mercury is an entirely different situation. The tendency is to inject more insulin, thinking a deficiency is present. There is actually a malfunction – toxic contamination – but, just like your own insulin, new insulin is not immune to being attacked by mercury. Consider removing the source of the malfunction instead of encouraging the situation by compensating for it.

The Big Guns – Estrogen and Testosterone

So much for the minor modifying hormones. Now let's look at the big guns. The major hormones that take control of your daily life.

Estrogen and testosterone. These two hormones comprise the Androgynic Factor. The strongest influence your mind faces each day. This is the pair that determines who you get along with and who you don't. This is the pair that can create the worst birth defects if violated. Therefore, males and females of identical endocrine patterns cannot tolerate being near each other, much less procreating.

> These two hormones comprise the Androgynic Factor.

There are exceptions, but only for short term relationships, and even that depends upon the degree of distance from the midline. This system is not like a scale of one to ten, but more like a gauge with zero in the middle (midline) and andric on one side and gynic on the other side.

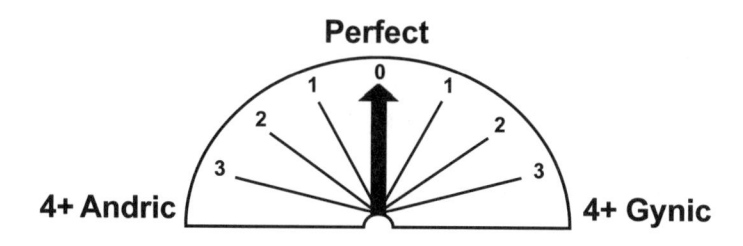

Perfect

4+ Andric **4+ Gynic**

All males and all females produce *both* estrogen *and* testosterone. Obviously, the male produces more testosterone, and the female more estrogen, but within the two sexual systems, either male or female can produce more estrogen or testosterone than meets the midline standard.

Page coined two terms to identify these excesses and deficiencies. A person, male or female, who produces more testosterone than is optimum for his/her sex is termed "andric" (pronounced ann - drick), from the root word androgen or the "male household". If they produce more estrogen than is ideal, they are termed "gynic" (pronounced gen - ick), from the same root that the word gynecology comes from. The balances / imbalances look something like this:

All males and all females produce both estrogen and testosterone. Obviously the male more testosterone and the female more estrogen.

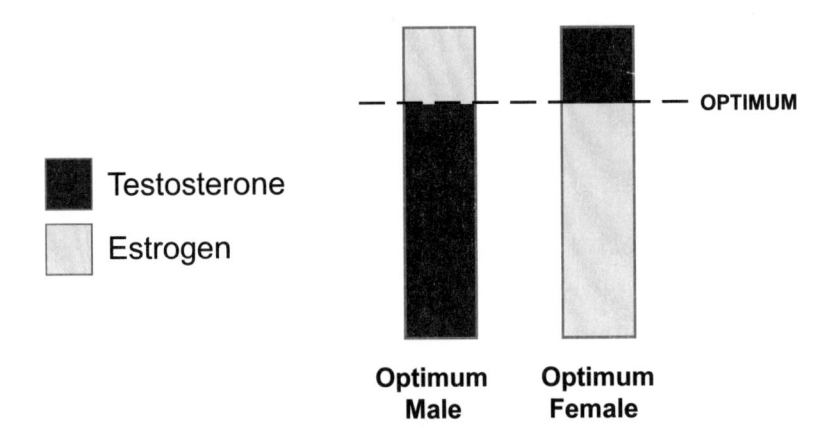

■ Testosterone
☐ Estrogen

Optimum Male   Optimum Female   — OPTIMUM

But, within the two, excesses and deficiencies can occur. Excess testosterone – relative to each sex – is termed andric. Excess estrogen is termed gynic.

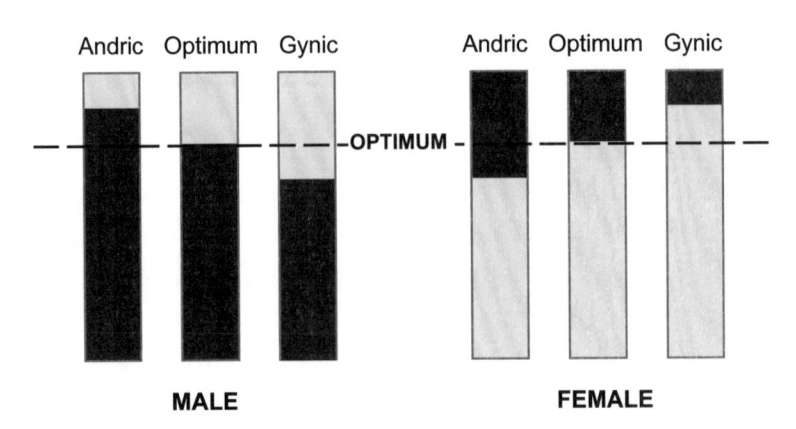

Andric   Optimum   Gynic   Andric   Optimum   Gynic

—OPTIMUM—

MALE   **FEMALE**

Estrogen and testosterone are the most influential hormones – the ones that react instantly during personal interactions between one person and another. When I was a Page student, there were about 50% andrics and 50% gynics in both male and female populations. Playing the odds, each person had a chance of finding an equal and opposite endocrine mate. Over the past three and a half decades, there has been a shift. We now note about 65% of the females are andric and about 65% of the males are gynic, so there is still a balance in favor of finding a mate, but this also indicates that we are rapidly heading toward a matriarchal-dominated society.

> *Estrogen and testosterone react instantly during personal interactions.*

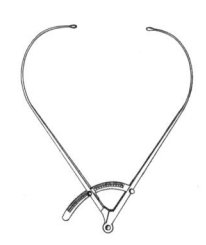

Page used the measurements of shoulders and hips performed with obstetrical calipers – bony measurements – as his primary source of determining the Androgynic Factor in his patients. Other measurements were good, but this bone to bone measurement was more accurate more of the time.

The shoulder measurement is taken by pressing the calipers firmly onto the shoulder bone. That is a little tough, because it feels like there are two shoulder bones.

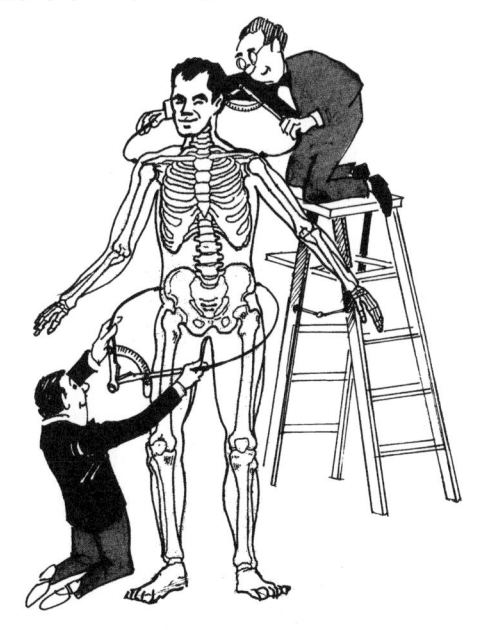

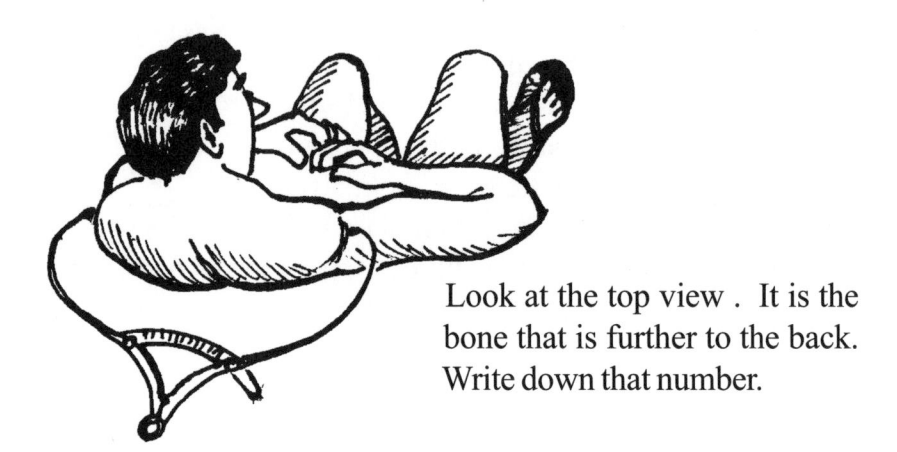

Look at the top view. It is the bone that is further to the back. Write down that number.

Next measure the distance from the top of the hip called the iliac crest. Have the patient point to their belly button, because the iliac crest is at the same level. Press firmly. Write this number down.

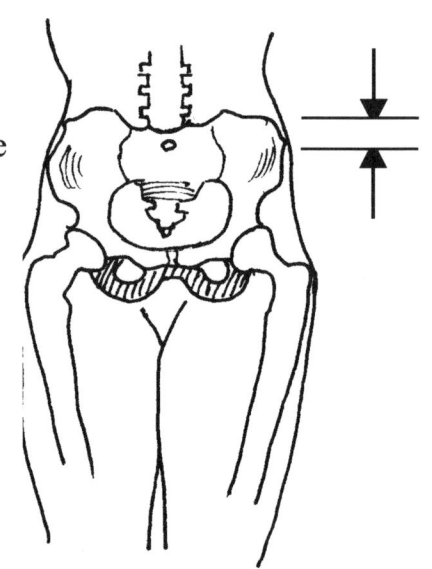

The shoulder measurement will be larger than the hip. Divide the hip measurement into the shoulder measurement.

The optimum points are:

    Male   = 1.346
    Female = 1.234

If the male shoulder divided by hip measurement is greater than 1.346, then he is andric. If the measurement is less than 1.346, he is gynic.

If the female measurement is greater than 1.234, she is andric. If less than 1.234, she is gynic.

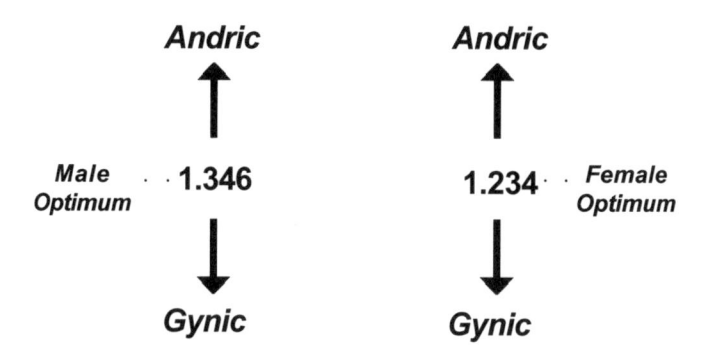

Andric ↑ Male Optimum · · 1.346 ↓ **Gynic**

Andric ↑ 1.234 · · Female Optimum ↓ **Gynic**

Page's treatment involved using minute doses of estrogen in the andric (male or female) to achieve balance as shown in the serum phosphorus levels. You may recall that low serum phosphorus levels are associated with disease progression, while proper phosphorus levels (close to 4 milligrams percent, but at least above 3.6) are indicative of regeneration. In the case of phosphorus, 3.5 mg% is the dividing line between degeneration and regeneration.

> *Page's treatment involved using minute doses of estrogen in the andric (male or female) to achieve balance as shown in the serum phosphorus levels.*

Equal and opposite.

Page used minute doses of testosterone to correct the low serum phosphorus levels in gynics. We are talking fractions of a milligram. The better correction he achieved, the less dental decay the person would have, and the better improvement they would see in degenerative or autoimmune diseases. And the more emotionally stable.

Andric *** Gynic

For the most part, what I shall present here are the <u>polar ends</u> of reactions of andrics and gynics.

Fortunately, there are very few totally andric or totally gynic people on the planet. What a mess that would be. Remember, the best place to be is in the center.

There are very few people in this area either, but this is our target. Our goal. A person in the center can play either the andric or gynic role successfully.

Typical 4+ Andric

The more andric a person, the more dominant, and the more gynic, the more passive. The more centered, the better ability to adjust to the requirements of the situation. Centered people can become dominant or passive depending on the situation and the desired outcome. They will also experience better health, emotional stability, and ability to get along in almost any situation of personal interaction, no matter how weird the other folks.

Dr. Page had a scale. One to four. He rated andrics and gynics on a scale starting at zero: the perfect balance.

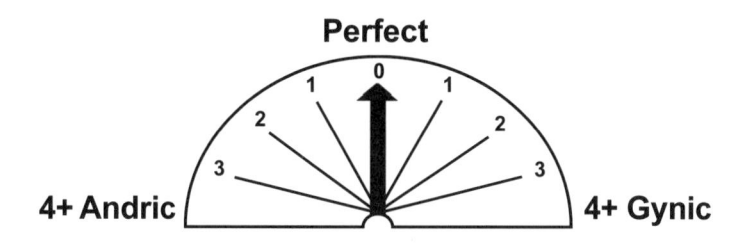

Perfect

4+ Andric **4+ Gynic**

The more andric a person, the closer to the dreaded 4+ andric. The more gynic, the closer to 4+ gynic. Both scales seem to go up, not equal and opposite.

Where one needed to use caution was the 4+ andric. They are more apt to take control and be argumentative. As the saying goes, "seldom right, but never in doubt". That may be a little severe, but it is not real far off the mark. 4+ andrics can be pretty smart, intuitive people, but they are never in doubt of their opinion being correct. Absolutely correct. The 4+ gynic would take advice and follow it to the letter – later. The gynic would prefer to have instructions written, for that is the way they learn best. The 4+ andric could be a good patient as far as compliance was concerned — if he understood exactly *why* he had to do what he was directed to do. Otherwise, why bother?

That was the great thing about body chemistry in treating andrics. Here is the perfect blood value Mr. or Mrs. Andric, and here is where you are. This explains your disease, and here is what you have to do to move from point X of disease to point Y of health if your desire is for better health. By the way, we will be taking another blood test in 6 days to see how well you are doing. Andrics like that. Competition with *themselves* is both challenging and rewarding. And there is a mark to achieve – short term – and determined by a machine – not an opinion. Hey! Let's go for it.

We would also tell the andric that the blood test was a two edged sword. If I mis-diagnose, or mis-calculate dosages or diet — the chemistry would tell on me. On the other hand, if you – Mr. or Mrs. Andric – mess up and do not follow the program – the chemistry tells on *you*. We are equally under the independent gun, but YOU are in control, because we teach *you* how to evaluate the chemistries. Hey, again. Andrics like to be in the pilot's seat, or at least be co-pilot.

> *The blood test was a two edged sword.*

Gynics are pretty well sold on being treated prior to asking for treatment. They do not have to be "hit over the head" in order to follow instructions. They generally have confidence in the person they have selected for treatment, because they have already checked him out thoroughly.

Let's look at the Androgynic Factor divided somewhat into reactions to situations. Keep in mind that I am presenting the *polar ends* of andric and gynic reactions. Most of us are more toward the middle, reflecting some of each behavior, but we can feel tendencies toward our personal poles if we are honest with ourselves.

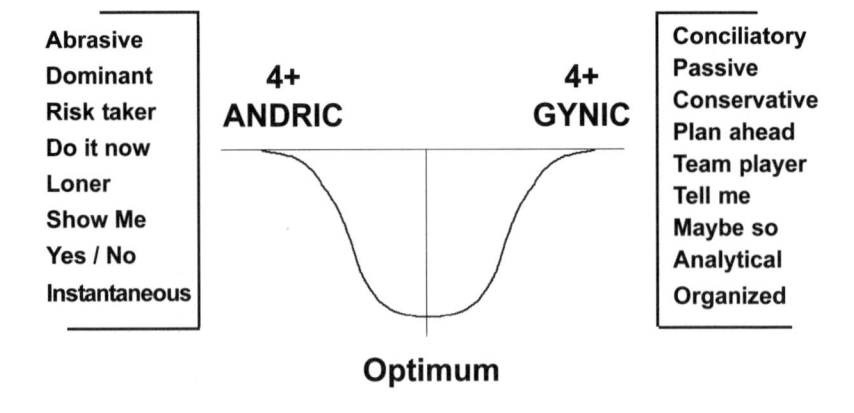

Abrasive Dominant Risk taker Do it now Loner Show Me Yes / No Instantaneous	**4+** **ANDRIC**	**4+** **GYNIC**	Conciliatory Passive Conservative Plan ahead Team player Tell me Maybe so Analytical Organized

Optimum

Andric - Gynic Habits?

Andrics like direct questions and direct answers. Gynics tend to get on the defensive when questioned. For example:

Andric male husband: "Honey, when will dinner be ready?" His agenda is that he needs to bring some papers up from the basement, and it will take 10 minutes to do that, which might interfere with her dinner schedule. His antenna is up for a number: 5, 10, 15 minutes, upon which his decision can easily be made.

Response from gynic female wife: "I had to pick up the kids, take Tommy to his music lesson, Sally to dance class, the grocery store was busy, and besides they didn't have any Redbird chicken, so I had to go to Albertson's on the other side of town, and by then both kids were ready and upset with me for not being on time, and I am just now cutting up the chicken."

"<u>How</u> long?" he reiterates with a bit of huffiness in his voice, his needs not having been met.

"If you think you can do this any faster than I can, then you come out here and do it yourself. Maybe you could at least set the table. That wouldn't hurt you. Just because your mother was a fast cook, just remember, you were an only child and she didn't have to look after the needs of two kids."

Is this going to lead to a congenial chicken dinner? Whose fault was it? No one's. It is a difference in perception. Needs were not met, because neither party understood what their partner's needs were. Each evaluated the situations in light of how they perceive reality.

He was not criticizing her. She was not the target she perceived she was. He was trying to be helpful by not messing up her dinner time, but war ensued due to a "lack of understandable communication". They really <u>were</u> communicating, just on different frequencies. Get on the understanding frequency of the Androgynic Factor, and life runs far more smoothly.

Now he could have stated his reasons for wanting to know how long before dinner. However, andrics do not generally *feel* the necessity of explaining their actions, for decisions are not usually based on verbal forms. They see mental pictures of actions. They do not hear words like the gynic thinks in. Gynics think in terms of total explanations, and, as in this case, take offense very easily if they perceive their actions or motives are not perfect. Gynics think in terms of lists of reasons why things are the way they are. They feel compelled to expound on those reasons. Andrics need only the bottom line.

> *Gynics think in terms of total explanations... and reasons why things are the way they are.*

> *Andrics do not generally feel the necessity of explaining their actions.*

If he were aware of the Androgynic Factors involved, he could have said:

"I need to bring up some files from the basement. Would it interfere with your dinner schedule if I took ten minutes to do that?"

If she understood that all he needed was a yes / no answer, she might have responded:

"No, I'm about 20 minutes from serving anyway, so go ahead."

That's if they both understood each other's hormones. Remember, they are still equal and opposite, just ignorant of each other's methods of establishing agendas.

There are many more stories that demonstrate methods of mis-communication, but that one covers the basics. Andrics want yes-no answers. Gynics feel compelled to defend. Equal and opposite.

As a very general view of polar andrics and gynics, consider the following section on descriptive characteristics.

General Characteristics

***Andrics** are instant decision makers – based more on gut reactions than analytical decisions.*

***Gynics** are laid back and analytical – make decisions by thinking over all the facts and evaluating them.*

Andrics are dominant, instant decisions makers, while gynics are laid back and analytical. Gynics make decisions by thinking over *all* of the facts and then evaluating them. They work with mental scales. If something has 4 advantages and 5 disadvantages, gynics vote against it. Andrics make instant decisions based more on gut reactions than analytical decisions. An andric says "yes", and, if you ask why, his answer is apt to be, "I said yes, what do you mean, why? Yes is my decision." A gynic could spend ten minutes explaining in great detail why he made his decision. It was a five to four vote. Of course I voted against it. It is a matter of mathematics and logic. Andrics don't always know why they made the decision, they just make decisions based on gut reactions.

Andrics tend to be more "sympathetic dominant" as far as their autonomic nervous system is concerned. Gynics are "parasympathetic dominant". For this reason andrics are often accused of having 'type A' behavior. Probably true. Gynics are known to be more laid back, non-volatile and thoughtful. I suppose this is type B.

Just what is type A and B behavior, and how does it differ from the Androgynic Factor? I found some information about this in James Gleick's recent book, *FSTR*, which is short for faster. "Type A" was coined by a pair of cardiologists (Dr. Meyer Friedman and Dr. Ray Rosenman) at a time when the public was trying to find a word to describe people who were excess hurriers bent on heart disease. There wasn't much science behind the observation, but the term filled a void and stuck. These cardiologists listed a set of personality traits which tended to be present in people who had heart disease. They were dubbed a group of competitive, aggressive people who had a "harrying sense of time urgency".

James Gleick comments on their finding by saying, "In reality, three decades of attention from cardiologists and psychologists have failed to produce any carefully specified and measurable set of character traits that predict heart disease – or to demonstrate that people who change their Type A behavior will actually lower their risk of heart disease."

Now I can see that there is a good reason for not finding something measurable to separate Type A from Type B. There is none – where they are looking. Heart disease is not the result of just traits. What they observed was the *result* of many factors, not the cause. From Page's aspect, we should consider excess testosterone as a contributor, the hyper thyroid as another contributor, and the hyper anterior pituitary is definitely influential, as is the intake of sugar, alcohol and caffeine. And don't forget the toxic influence of mercury from common silver fillings, nickel from crowns, and the ever destructive root canal. There is no one single predictive factor. It is all accumulative and related to one's genetic ability to survive. All are factors, and all are important.

> *Altering one's behavior does not alter one's chemistry.*

And certainly altering one's behavior does not alter one's chemistry or genetic potential to react to given situations. If a car speeding at 90 miles an hour makes a 20 degree turn to the left, it is still speeding at 90 miles an hour. Behavior modification is an attempt to copy something that our endocrines may fight. Like Popeye says, "I yam what I yam." But, through education, we can recognize what we are and <u>adapt</u> different methods of dealing with situations in more socially acceptable ways. However, this assumed adaptation creates a whole new different type of stress that can lead to the originally intended heart attack, for, internally, our chemistry is still guiding our physiological reactions. If we add to this alteration of dietary intake, there is less stress on our system. If we correct the imbalances of our endocrine system, we can adapt even better. But, if we change behavior by copying an unnatural behavior and not attending to the other stressors, change by copying can eventually lead to disease. We do need to control our original steam pressure by reducing its hormonal and dietary causes, or by finding some accepted method of defusing excess energy. Copy cat is part of the answer, but recognition of root causes has to be considered as well.

Andrics are interested in instant gratification. Velcro would exemplify their behavior. Clothing manufacturers have missed the boat for andric purchasing trends. Andrics would prefer having everything open or close with Velcro. Gynics are the ones that can tolerate a dress with 35 buttons on it, because it is stylish. Gynics take more time in dressing for the occasion, for it is worth it to them to make the proper fashion statement.

> *Andrics are interested in instant gratification. Velcro would exemplify their behavior.*

> *Gynics match color, texture, complementary colors, current style of acceptance and cost.*

Fashion statement? When buying for himself, an andric male may buy a tie "because I like it" even when he has absolutely nothing that matches it. Gynics match color, texture, complementary colors, current style of acceptance and cost. If an andric likes it, cost is superficial, as long as it is within reason.

Andrics shop for convenience. Gynics do comparison shopping with quality and cost carefully interwoven. Gynics are always thinking in terms of the complete outfit, not just the tie.

Gynics are peace makers looking for mid-ground. They do not mind taking a few more minutes, or even hours, to discuss something if the outcome is peaceful. Andrics tend to be abrasive and sarcastic when verbally crossing swords with someone.

Gynics tend to be investors. They don't like being out on a limb. They like to live "by the book". Comfort to them is the security of repetition. It is more predictive. Andrics tend to be creative risk takers, especially about their own ideas.

Even though andrics are not outstanding in social skills, they do like the sensuous. They like the feel of cashmere, chinchilla, the taste of fine wines. They would sooner not drink a wine they do not care for than drink one they don't like, despite who the hostess is. Gynics know how to say the polite thing to the hostess; they are the ones to bring small gifts to her. They see to it that notes of appreciation are sent after the party.

Andrics may like Paganini, Scarlotti, Mozart, the great bombastic symphonies of Beethoven that provide the "symphony reaction" of goose bumps. Music that makes a statement. Gynics may prefer sonatas, Pacobel, Glenn Miller, mood music, background music that andrics may find interruptive.

Andrics may be emotionally high strung and aggressive, but not brutal. They are more apt to cry at movies, to choke up on emotional stories. Although active and controlled during emotional crises when they occur, they may cry on recounting the adventure.

Gynics can control their external emotions. They can be the ministers at a

> *Gynics can control their external emotions.*

funeral of their relative or a good friend, and speak in a controlled voice that does not get choked up over the emotion of the moment. That does not mean they do not feel the emotion. They are highly complex emotional individuals. They just have a better ability to "control" their emotions when it is socially more acceptable.

Show ✲✲✲ *and* ✲✲✲ *Tell*

This is a major difference between andric and gynic learning methods. Andrics are monkey-see, monkey-do type of people. Show me – visually. Let me watch. They are not ones to be found reading directions before assembling items from the home building stores. That is for the gynic. Tell the gynic how to do something, and he can probably visualize and accomplish it. If he has some trouble, give him some written directions. Gynics can read and relate to instructions – even maps – and derive knowledge of how to accomplish a task. Andrics learn by trial and error or observation. Gynics do not make nearly as many errors, but andrics seem to have more fun trying to assemble by creativity – even if the final product does not look like the picture on the box. Gynics will not stop until the final product matches all of its requirements – and looks identical to the picture on the box.

Our school systems are set up almost entirely for gynic learning abilities. Readin', writin' and 'rithmatic. Mostly reading. Only kindergarten has kids *doing*. Even colleges are centered on lecturers. With the exception of laboratory. Who makes the best scores in lecture exams? In laboratory exams? Ever think of that? Is it really a fair assessment of learning ability to average them together for a cumulative single grade?

The only activity an andric finds in grade school is during recess. The rest of the time he is expected to sit still, listen and learn. There are three things that are not compatible with his developing mind. When an andric finds himself in an intolerable situation, he usually bails out rather than trying to negotiate a settlement or compromise. That is why the high school drop outs are primarily andrics. They found no challenge or reward that met their specific andric needs. They are not impressed with paper awards, badges, medals and the like. They need personal gratification that they actually *did* something. Personal accomplishment matters. If they are lucky, maybe they have a year of "shop" in which they can take out their creativity on pieces of metal and wood. It may not take any ribbons, but they accomplished something *tangible*. That is the type of satisfaction they crave in order to continue to develop and learn.

Gynics have high regard for education as it is taught in the US. Gynics are comfortable with reading and repeating what they learned. They tend to make the higher scholastic marks on written exams. They yearn for higher education, and frequently aim for the highest degree possible in their field.

Music lessons? Divided. Again, andrics and gynics can both play musical instruments, but they learn differently. I know a woman who has played accomplished piano for over 50 years, yet can play nothing without music in front of her. Gynic? I have personally heard andrics learning to play musical instruments. Learn to count? Yeah, sure. You can hear them scrambling around through the notes, with very little correctness in transference from paper to sound. But, let the scamps talk the teacher into playing it once, and all of a sudden, it is like they instantly learned to read music. Not really. They are playing by "ear". The ability to monkey-see, monkey-do applies here, only as monkey-*hear*, monkey-do. Only then does the written music take on meaning. They must hear the musical expression before they can mimic it. Then, later, they may be able to place their own signature of creativity to the music, but the initial learning is not always done well by looking at ink notes on a piece of paper.

Check out the symphony orchestras. Almost all of the musicians will be gynic. A few stray andrics will be found, but the true connoisseur of music and its proper presentation belongs to the gynic.

How many virtuosos or accomplished musicians have never developed because of having to practice the scales? What would happen if you taught an andric child to play the melody of a popular song that all of his buddies knew, rather than the difference between A major and A minor? Might he develop a new self respect in front of his peers? What might that lead to? Is it possible for one to play an instrument who doesn't really know what A is? Remember, andrics will fight valiantly to achieve what they desire. Gynics may fight valiantly to achieve what their parents or teachers want, but that never motivates the andric. Andrics must be given reason to build desire.

At the bottom line, people who play in the orchestra, or who become the virtuosos of the day – are gynics. Andrics greatly appreciate music and can tell if a note is missed, or if a phrase is superb, but they are more satisfied to listen to the accomplished gynic who has spent endless hours capturing that ability to perform. Gynics prefer to criticize each other's talents – or lack thereof. Andrics can more often love music without reservation.

Who among us does not have a need for someone to help us when the car won't start? When the roof leaks? When we need "service" beyond what we learned reading, writing and calculating. Why not train people in services? What they used to call "trade schools". Gynics voted those schools down, because they were manual as compared with cerebral. We need both. Why force a square peg into a round hole when he could be learning something useful to himself and to society?

Would that reduce crime? Think about it. Ambitious andrics fall in love with television ads just like everyone else. If they do not have a salable skill to help them earn those desires, then why not just take what you want? Chances of getting caught are only about 5%, so go for it. Almost gynic logic. Both andrics and gynics get involved in the crime world. Andrics find the potential loot, gynics do the planning, and ask the andrics to implement the crime while the gynic keeps the engine running in the get away vehicle.

But what if they do get caught? What then? Gynics plead for forgiveness and feign remorse. The gynic judge buys into it and the kid gets probation, community service and a mark on his paper record. It was worth it. Start planning the next one, but be more cautious. When the andric is brought before the judge, he is feeling anger at being confined in a cage. It's the worst thing you can do to an andric. This is definitely counter-rehabilitation. He is sarcastic and mouthy to the judge, telling him how he really feels. The gynic judge protects society by throwing the book at that incorrigible and tries to find a place for him that is more fool-proof in design than the andric's creativity in finding a way to escape.

Escape plans are sometimes brilliant. We are losing a lot of brain horsepower by incarcerating these andrics, especially in "solitary confinement". Boy. Talk about reforming. You are positively encouraging retaliation. Instead, put them somewhere where they have to pay for the damage they did, plus pay for their upkeep, by *producing* something in exchange, and they will understand that. They might even welcome the opportunity to learn a trade – especially by watching and experiencing.

Gun point? Here is a good word of advice. Andrics may be the first to draw a gun, they many flaunt it around and threaten, but they are not really apt to shoot you, unless threatened with no escape. Then, they may shoot. Their violence has its limitations. If you get caught, you get caught. Let's not make the situation any worse by killing somebody. If faced by both men and women with guns, do whatever the andric female tells you to do. With the slightest provocation, she *will* kill you. With no remorse. Gynic females are not fond of guns. Unless they were raised in Texas.

> *If faced with guns, do whatever the andric female tells you to do. With the slightest provocation, she will kill you.*

Voice? This is a casual observation, but it appears that andric women tend to have lower voice pitch, compounded by smoking cigarettes. In men, there is not a definite division, for very large gynic men can sing operatic tenor, or just as often bass. I have no idea what the difference is, but women are more apt to have higher voice registers if they are gynic, and lower tones if they are andric.

Business ★★★ Occupation

The best way for an andric to become president of a company is if he owns it. He is sometimes abrasive, makes decisions others do not understand, and moves too rapidly for gynics who like to "evaluate" situations.

CEO

Andric — I own the business

Gynic — I was unanimously elected

In meetings, the andric is guaranteed to interrupt. This is irritating to others, but if the andric doesn't get his new idea recognized and discussed right now, he will forget it — forever. And it might have been the best idea of the century.

> *In meetings, the andric is guaranteed to interrupt.*

Gynics rarely step on toes or interrupt, which logically wins them the presidency of the company. The ones chosen for awards. Whose pictures get in the newspapers. Gynics are dependable as clock work - and often about that creative and that interested in change.

> *Gynics rarely step on toes or interrupt.*

Andrics and gynics can both find jobs. Neither is good nor bad. But some people are more suited for some positions than others. The important thing is, *"who is working with whom?"*

Andrics tend to be happiest where protocol is not as important as being able to instantly evaluate a situation and create evasive maneuvers to correct the problem before it gets out of hand. Going by the book does not work for them, nor for the situations they can handle the best. Gynics are thinkers and planners. Evaluators of the long term significance of their decisions. Protocol. A pecking order of responsibility is super important for the gynic, for it assigns responsibility and leadership. Who is in charge. It draws lines in the sand over which one does not step. They are into detail. Great detail. They make good brain surgeons and equally good safe-crackers. Good and bad are not elements of decision in the Androgynic Factor. They just are.

Let's put the bottom line at the top in business. Andrics come up with good ideas, are strong starters – they usually want action today; but just short of the finish line, they lose interest. When they see that the goal is achievable, they start looking for the excitement of another new project.

Gynics make great support players. After the enthusiasm of the andric rubs off on the gynic, he becomes focused on the finish and can be counted on to tend to all the details and follow through so that the company can break the ribbon and win the race.

Andrics in business are *bottom line only* people. No holds barred. Go for the gold. Gynics know that nothing is as simple as going from point A to point B in a straight line. They are natural negotiators. They are ready for the interruptions and are good at negotiating around obstacles in order to achieve the goal with as little loss as possible. But! They know there will be losses and gains along the way and accept that as a way of life. Andrics see only the straight line from A to B and get irritated with variances. They attack variances with a vengeance, but want errors pointed out immediately so quick correction can reestablish the straight line course again.

When an andric is interested in his business, he is apt to be *passionately* interested. He spends most of his waking hours creating new ideas. His secretary probably has been heard saying, "I never know what I am going to do from day to day. Each morning when he comes in (and God only knows what time that will be), he will rearrange the priorities, and, 'by the way, here is a new project to institute by noon today'." Never boring around an andric boss. Possibly frustrating in an office where there is a place for everything and everything in its place type of secretary, but they like each other. They are equal and opposite and feed off of each other's strengths.

Andrics have a big problem in business – they trust people.

Andrics have a big problem in business. They trust people on their own personal evaluation. If they don't like a person on first introduction, hang it up. Permanently. But, for the most part, andrics think the majority of folks are honest. Especially if they have the same apparent interests. They are comfortable doing large business deals on a handshake. Hark! There are unscrupulous people out there.

Gynics are good at forming business strategies.

How do I know? Just ask a gynic. They tend to look suspiciously at everyone in business. They are apt to say: "Prove it. Show me the data. Show me the money." Boy, does an andric CEO need a gynic advisor. In most cases both people are wrong. The vendor is not as honest as the andric thinks, and not as evil as the gynic thinks. But, if the andric is smart, he will let the gynic evaluate the actual product (not just the claims), call other people the vender has dealt with, get references, personal, business and financial. Write contracts longer than the Bill of Rights. In short, protect the CEO *and* the business both before and after the transaction. That is the gynic's job. Anticipate litigation.

The gynic advisor may have to play a bit of andric role and push the andric CEO around in order to get things wrapped up securely while he is trying to assign employees to their new tasks even before the contract is signed. Who wants to be in business anyway? Both andrics and gynics, but for different reasons.

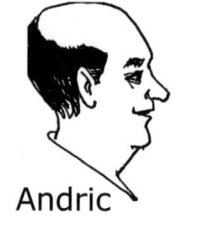

Andrics make decisions based on overviews and general assessments. If the decision has to do with money, tell him to the closest thousand. Do not confuse the issue with hundreds, tens or for heaven's sake, never mention pennies.

An andric usually remembers two figures. Probably the last two he hears. If an andric boss is ready to make a buy / don't buy decision, he needs to know how much money is in the bank account. He asks the gynic accountant for a balance and receives an answer like "twenty-six-thousand-two-hundred-fourteen-dollars-and-thirty-six-cents". The andric remembers the number 36.

No, how much money is in the bank in <u>round</u> figures? "26 thousand two hundred fourteen dollars," says the gynic.

What the andric wants to hear is, "a little over 26 thousand".

"Well, that's not entirely accurate," replies the gynic accountant.

"But it tells me whether or not we can afford to buy this piece of equipment," replies the andric. The gynic goes away feeling that the boss is not watching things as closely as he should, and the andric thinks that the accountant is so involved in penny trees that he cannot see the dollar forest.

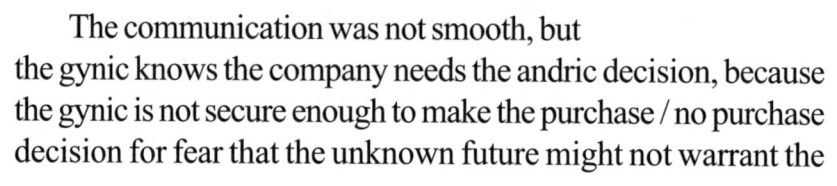

The communication was not smooth, but the gynic knows the company needs the andric decision, because the gynic is not secure enough to make the purchase / no purchase decision for fear that the unknown future might not warrant the expenditure in returns. There might be a loss, and it would be on his shoulders. Gynic shoulders do not like to risk failure, even if success would reap great rewards. Nothing wrong with status quo. The andric has a gut feeling that the market is going to move in that direction and wants to be ready to satisfy the demand when it hits. He does NOT want to start after the competition has figured it out and moved into his sales territory. By that time he has lost his competitive advantage of being the firstest with the mostest.

Gynics are good at forming business strategies. They can also design logistics to go with the strategies. Then they should pick an andric to implement the actions. Especially the logistics. Logistics have to be flexible on a moment's notice in order to keep the strategy front and center. Flexibility does not fit the gynic mind, but fulfilling the strategies does. Gynics are smart if they allow the andric flexites latitude to go with the flow, and keep their own focus on the overall strategy. Then the andric must be ready to put a gynic in place at the end of the excitement part of the project to make sure all the ribbons are tied.

Henry Ford preferred to work with gynic males. He wanted people who thought things out before acting. He had a unique way of separating andrics from gynics at interviews. Ford would take them to lunch. If the prospect salted his food before tasting it – he was out. If he tasted first, then added salt, he was in. There is a sound Androgynic principle behind this. Andrics require more protein, and protein requires salt for proper digestion. Andrics have learned over the years that gynics prepare most of the restaurant food, and require less salt than andrics. Therefore, they salt their prepared foods less. "Why waste one good bite?" is the subliminal andric thought when

Gynic

salting food prior to tasting. Andrics know the food will need more salt, the only question is how much more? Ford got his gynics. Thinkers and planners.

Andrics do well on short term projects that require lots of intense, focused input and dedication for a few months – few weeks would be even better. Gynics are in for the long haul. Gynics are the ones who invented the self-evaluation forms that include your one year plan, 5 year plan, 10 year plan. Andrics would sarcastically add, what about the 50 year projection? Andrics have no idea of their one year plan, except in generalities, like graduate from school, and that, hopefully, next year will be a lot different from today. How? Matters not. "Just bring me a different set of challenges," says the andric.

Gynics vote for safe corporate investments. Investments where there is a past history that indicates stability of decisions, and a constant profit margin. Andrics leap to the future with all stops pulled out. Go for the gold.

Gynic decisions are "methodical" and based on lots of research looking for stability. Andric decisions are more apt to be based on gut reactions to bottom line information.

In business situations, andrics are not apt to be "understanding" about slip-ups that happened because someone was asleep at the switch. An andric's solution to a real screw up because of inattention to your job is, "You're fired." If, however, an error occurs that was just a plain honest mistake, tell the andric boss about it quickly, and he will probably try to correct it post-haste before it becomes a big disaster. He will then compliment you for bringing it to his attention before it got out of hand. Don't try to cover things up around an andric. They can face problems and mistakes, but cannot handle smoothing over the situation and pretending that it didn't happen.

To andrics, it is the final result that counts. How you get there is inconsequential. Gynics are far more interested in protocol. Was it followed? Did you do it by the book?

On a personal note, I published a paper on ridding spinal fluid of abnormal proteins in Multiple sclerosis patients within 12 days. All of the wheelchair bound MS patients were able to stand and take a few steps before the 12th day. I was elated. I thought this result was fantastic. I expected commentary from the article. I got one comment — "Did the patients sign permission forms before the spinal taps?"

"Yes, they did." I asked if he wanted the detailed protocol we had used, if he wanted to try it on MS patients, wanted hand-holding during the procedures?

"Heavens no. I never see patients. I am a university professor, and just wanted to make sure your program was properly conducted." The protocol was more important than the final result. "We can't have people out there doing things that are not properly conducted."

My andric (non-verbal) reply was, we need <u>someone</u> out there <u>doing</u> something that helps these people. Polar opposite thinking. Who is correct? Both.

Gynics make great accountants. They can work on columns of figures from 8 till 5 and go home very satisfied with their performance. (By the way, they leave at 5:01 every day, and arrive home at 5:26 every day.) They may not remember the numbers from the day, but the important thing is that they balanced. Pennies are very important to the gynic, for without them, they cannot balance to the penny. Andrics do not even like to balance their own checkbooks, but have an uncanny sense of how much is in their account. To the nearest hundred.

Computer programmers tend to be gynics. They follow or invent logic very well. Andrics might challenge the logic of some things, since andrics are more time-motion conscious.

Conservation of energy seems to be an over-riding emotion. Take the computer screens for word processing, for example. In some programs, the lower right hand corner tells you about what line you are in to the hundredth, and position on that line to the hundredth. It does have one piece of andric information. What page am I on? Andrics would rather know what page relative to the whole document than the hundredth of an inch of where I am on the line. They can see that.

In order to "save", you go to the upper *left* part of the screen. Then to "close", you go to the upper *right*. Then to shut down, you drop all the way to the *lower left* to hit "start", then up a notch to confirm your intentions, then hit a button there and another shut down icon appears above the middle of the screen. "That's so the computer can be sure you really want to go on to another project." Computer? "What about me?" asks the andric. "I'm the guy ready to go to another project, or I would not have started the shut down sequence. Why not just hit the same place three times? Look at all that time and energy wasted in travel." (Do computers award frequent flyer miles?) The gynic would retort, "I never noticed that, but who is it that shuts things down and forgets to 'save'?" Yes, that is apt to be the andric getting in too much of a hurry.

Airline pilots. They had better be gynic. In airline pilot training, pilots are grilled on all the possible things that could go wrong. They practice reflex action in simulators. They think about where the closest airport is at all times, just in case. They constantly practice thinking of all the possibilities for the unanticipated. Most of the time, when they are working, they are on automatic pilot. This would drive an andric nuts. Sitting and doing nothing but anticipating disaster while a computer does the flying. Not very creative. But, when the problem occurs, gynics can reflexively take care of them, for they have practiced for these events for years. They live hours of boredom interrupted by moments of sheer panic, but have the reflexes to handle problems should they arrive.

Andric pilots? There should be a law. Andrics would tend to take off, head the plane toward its destination, then fasten their seat belts and check the fuel gauge. Flight plans? Just a suggestion from which the real trip will be altered as the flight goes on. Let the gynic males – and andric females – fly the airplanes.

Whenever a female steps into a time honored male role, remember, it is going to be an andric female. Andric female pilots will work twice as hard in the detail area as their gynic male counterparts, because they know they cannot fail. When an andric becomes passionate, watch out. There is nothing they will not learn or practice to achieve a <u>self-set goal</u> with a reason behind it. That is why you find the occasional andric surgeon, dentist, pilot, or lawyer (though I have never heard of one). For some reason, they want this type of challenge and will put an enormous amount of effort into accomplishing it.

I have seen inadvertent violations of the Androgynic Factor destroy great ideas.

Here's the scenario: An andric dentist (rare, but it happens 15% of the time) gets a brilliant idea. He approaches two gynic dentists with his brainchild. "Why don't we consolidate our three practices? There is space available near here, so patient traffic won't be a problem. Let's pool our equipment, sell the duplicates and use that money for the move. We would need only one secretary instead of three, one accountant instead of three, equipment for six operatories instead of 8, 6 assistants instead of 8, less X-ray equipment, could take advantage of large purchase discounts, and the best part: we can all make the same amount of money working 4 days a week that we used to in 5.

Andric

We can cover the entire practice one weekend every three instead of individually every weekend. Fewer personnel to juggle, fewer headaches, far fewer expenses, better group rate insurance policies. It will be great."

Sounds logical. The gynics buy into it. The new practice is set up and running. After two weeks, there are unforeseen problems. Two assistants formerly from one of the gynics' offices quit because they don't like working with a different dentist (just happens to be the andric). The andric dentist fires a third assistant from a gynic dentist's former office. Remember, andric males and andric females cannot work together in a close environment like doctor-assistant. The gynic receptionist formerly with the andric dentist cannot collect money from clients because it makes her uncomfortable. The andric dentist always set up the financial arrangements. She gets fired by the gynic dentists, because they see the finances going "south". The andric dentist gets miffed, because the secretary has been with him 6 years, and they had a good working relationship.

Gynic

"She can learn," the andric defends her. Oh, no, she can't. She can't ask for money any better than the two gynic dentists who have depended on an andric secretary to do "the dirty work". Gynics like to manage money, but asking for it is uncomfortable, therefore, dirty.

After a couple of years of in-fighting for no "apparent" reason, the practice dissolves into bankruptcy and mutual lawsuits seeking vainly to place blame. The blame was that it was unworkable from the endocrine standpoint to start with. Had all three dentists been either andric or gynic, and had they hired a now-affordable andric manager working with a now-affordable gynic accountant, the concept would have worked well. Throw that immiscible bunch of nice folks together, however, and there is no way the system can survive.

Female truck drivers, steam roller operators, soldiers, policewomen, race car drivers, women libbers. They all have excess testosterone relative to the ideal female. They are andrics. They are more comfortable in traditional male roles. Not that they are masculine – just andric.

Psychologists and ministers. Almost all are gynics. All bent on helping their fellow man. Necessary? You bet. I have a lot of respect for both professions, and, in good andric fashion, have some advice that would increase their success rate. Suppose they are amenable to an outsider presenting what was never mentioned in school?

Who gets in trouble? Usually the andric for *non-compliance*. Gynics do not understand the andric instant responses and therefore label them irresponsible. Andrics frequently get sent to "counselors". Seldom go, but frequently get referred. Not new, for they used to get sent to the Principal for the same reasons.

> *Gynics do not understand the andric instant responses.*

If a gynic goes to a counselor, the conversation can be quite organized and logical. The problem can logically be analyzed by "an outsider", and solutions will become obvious. A logical set of new patterns can be suggested, and the case will have a high potential for success. Makes everyone feel good.

When an andric goes to a counselor, the counselor cannot get a logical response as to what made the andric do what he did. The andric just did. He did not plan the event, he just did it.

"Well, how did you *feel* about it?" is the routine question.

Feel? Gynics work on feelings. Andrics do not. Ask an andric about how he feels, and he may describe a headache or sprained ankle. Feelings to the andric are physical things. Things that are handled by an aspirin. To a gynic counselor, they are emotions. Language barrier.

The counselor tries to set up a new pattern of behavior. Based on what? On his own gynic behavior patterns that work well for him. Try logic, planning, evaluating, looking at both sides. Weighing things in the balance. Andrics see only one side. The side requiring action. And that is determined by what needs to be done. Now! Not on a mathematical time wasting decision, but on "now" decisions. Hey! Yes or no? Black or white? After a while into the counseling session, the andric may nod as if in agreement and promise several things so he can get out of there and on with his life. He needs freedom from this weird, surreal, imaginary environment. But this gobbledygook of logic, feeling, evaluating, making lists, consideration of your inner child's needs – look at, what was it – both sides? How many sides of a paper can you write on at once? There is only one side that shows.

Marriage counselors are also gynic. And boy, do they have problems. The counselors, that is. They try to set a pattern of conciliation, and it frequently fails. Why? Because you need two patterns of conciliation. One for the andric and another one for the gynic. But, most important, if the andric can be shown what makes the gynic tick, and the gynic be shown what makes the andric tick, then there can be mutual understanding. Each thinks the other is not seeing life correctly. And / but, they are both right.

There was a minister once who had two sons, ages 8 and 10. They got into an argument once in which Mother referred them to Father to settle the matter. The father listened to one boy, and concluded, "You are right, son." He then listened to the other boy's story, and concluded, "You are right, son." Out of sight, Mother had been listening to the conversations. She confronted the minister afterwards by saying, "Dear, they can't both be right." To which he responded, "You are right, too."

That's more of the situation in marriage disputes. They are both right, just from their own perspective. Andrics and gynics have different perceptions – and <u>perception is reality</u>.

Let's look at hospital employees.

Surgeons are gynics. End of the scale gynics. 4+. They can stand in one place for three hours carving on someone's brain and never whimper. Scrub nurses had better be 4+ andrics. They are responsible for seeing to it that all instruments are ready and in the doctor's hand two seconds before he knows he needs it. Even in emergency situations, they do not have to speak to each other. They already know what the other partner is thinking. They blend. They work as a team.

Andric

And the most andric of andrics is the head nurse. Scheduler of surgical events. She has to see to it that all personnel are present and trained properly. This is no time for pampering. Things must be done right!!! No exceptions.

The surgeon cannot be worrying about which instruments are ready and if they are sterile. If an instrument is missing, she has the head of the offender on a platter. That doctor has to have everything when he needs it. Secretly, she thinks he hung the moon. The gynic surgeon is thinking, boy, am I glad she is running things. Such efficiency. She is really something.

Now, they are not going to run off from their families and get married. They just have a truly deep respect and admiration for each other and their equal and opposite abilities. They are andric and gynic making a super team.

And the king of gynics? The anesthesiologist. They may be so gynic that they prefer no conversation with patients – or anyone else for that matter. In the dressing room, if they are not actively dressing, they probably have their nose buried in a medical journal. They will be polite enough toward their colleagues, but are not apt to initiate a conversation. The patient might ask them how they are at the first of the procedure, and they may converse like, "Take a deep breath and count backwards from 100. By nines." Soon, conversation will be limited to the noise of the gasses and scribbling of pen on paper as multiple measurements are recorded for posterity that will probably never be read. But, just in case.

The king of gynics is the anesthesiologist.

Gynic

There are cases of misplaced andrics and gynics. During my hospital externship I assisted an andric surgeon. Talk about oxymoron. This man could do a T & A (remove tonsils and adenoids) in about 8 minutes flat. Most other surgeons took closer to 20 minutes. His idea was that faster surgery meant less blood loss, less anesthetic to detoxify, less time before recovery and therefore better healing. He mentioned his time record to an anesthesiologist once in my presence, and got a really cold shouldered response. Something about too easy to make mistakes and he knew other fast surgeons anyway. No way was he going to compliment the fast surgeon for his achievement or goals he had accomplished. My heart went out to the surgeon, for he had just undergone a semi-dressing down in front of me – a lowly dental extern. I really liked the guy and could see what he was trying to do. He was good. Never made an unnecessary cut. Missed the small arteries and veins better than any of the other surgeons. Less tying off of "bleeders".

"Just jealousy," he commented, but I knew he was hurt internally, so I stayed around to let him chat for a while. Andrics may be brusque and move around fast, but they are delicate emotionally. When they step on toes, it is not with vicious intent. It is with conviction that another way is actually best. When gynics let you have it, they intend to cut to the core.

Team work is not only doctor-assistant, but also any place where people have to depend on someone of the opposite sex. Take "pairs" competition in ice skating for instance. She spins around in one direction, he in another, they come together, he catches her and tosses her into the air, from which she makes a perfect landing. WoW!! How do they do that? By thinking to each other. For that kind of precision, the two competitors must be equal and opposite in endocrine patterns, or all the training in the world will not yield them the championship. Andric and gynic are primary, but hypo and hyper thyroid would improve the match. And throw in a bit of active posterior pituitary for good emotional stability under stress. These folks do not have time to get their feelings hurt during an event.

> *Team work is also any-place where people have to depend on someone of the opposite sex.*

Ever wonder how trapeze artists flip through the air with the greatest of ease and catch each other? Who's watching whom?

Who is thinking about the safety net? I found the secret once in my dental operatory.

My assistant and I had worked together for 8 years. We had never had a cross word between ourselves and really enjoyed what we did together. She was a sit down comic, and I was the straight man. She entertained the patients while we did procedures without saying a word about what we were doing with sharp instruments.

One day we were in the operatory, each working on separate projects and there was no patient in the chair. I needed a pair of pliers to bend an orthodontic wire, and saw them sitting close to her.

"Would you please hand me that Baker 2?" I asked.

"Sure."

PLOP!

The pliers fell on the floor. We were both stupefied. Never in 8 years had we dropped an instrument. Never. We stared in horror at each other for a moment thinking of all the times that a dropped instrument could cause havoc.

"I'm sorry," she muttered. "I wasn't looking. In fact, I never look. I depend on you to look at the instruments."

"Me?" I said with equal amazement. "I never look either. My eyes are locked on the patient. I thought you were the one with perfect aim. It never occurred to me to think about looking at an instrument you were passing."

Then it dawned on me.

This was the Androgynic Factor at work. Neither of us watched or planned instrument passing. It just happened as we both viewed the same procedure – each thinking from a different prospective. I, thinking about what I was about to do now; she, about what I was going to do next. Just like ice skaters – the surgeon and nurse, the trapeze artists.

> *Neither of us watched or planned instrument passing.*
> *It just happened.*

Any well performing team must work with uncanny anticipation and mutual unplanned trust. No problem — if you have equal and opposite endocrine patterns.

On the personal financial front, gynics invest in blue chips, andrics tend to squander.

The andric can make lots of money in business, spend lots, gamble on himself and go broke more often than a gynic. But the andric rebounds without psychologically beating himself up. Expect him to swing from millionaire to near bankruptcy, but never to stay on an even keel. A gynic would suffer self-flagellation and remorse for making a wrong decision that lost money. Gynics may not make as much money as the andric does when he hits a mother load, but gynics may end up with more in the end times, because they tend to squirrel their money away and invest it wisely. At age 80, the gynic may have a huge amount of residual wealth, but is still reluctant to spend even small amounts of it on himself. He has spent a whole lifetime saving and investing and may not have learned how to spend. He may feel remorse at spending anything on himself, even if it could bring lots of happiness. It carves into his security thinking mind.

Assembly line operators have to have gynic characteristics. They can do repetitive operations with competence and feel satisfaction with the outcome in terms of numbers. Andrics will go nuts on assembly lines. They will try to find ways of improving the system, and, if that fails, they will go on to something that brings a new challenge every day. Or hour. Andrics need outlets for creativity and for drama. They do not do well with status quo.

Secure ⋆⋆⋆ Insecure

Andrics tend to be secure in about anything they tackle. If they are not secure, they avoid the subject entirely. You can't talk them into it. They are apt to be the one to introduce themselves to others at a party. They are hard people to sell insurance to. Yeah, yeah, they know the value and the risks, but call me tomorrow. Most insurance purchases are made based on insecurity or fear of the future. These are not common assets in andrics. They realistically understand the necessity of insurance, but are not apt to jump into the buy mode out of fear or insecurity. Factual information about the kids' college tuition and insurance as an investment to make sure it is paid – maybe that would get their attention. They are risk takers – up to a point. They are not ones to risk stepping into a boxing ring or do sky diving, but they are willing to invest in a new idea. Especially if it is their own. They don't mind risking being wrong and being laughed at for failure of their own new idea – ah, so what? As long as it involves an interesting challenge.

Andrics make great commission sales people. They are willing to "eat what they kill" in the marketplace. If they miss a sale, it's their fault. If they land a big one, they want their piece of the pie, and will not ask for a penny more. What's fair is fair. Win or lose. What is important to them is that they are in control and, therefore, are willing to accept feast or famine. The word insecurity is not in their vocabulary. They thrive on winning in the unknown.

> *Andrics are willing to "eat what they kill" in the marketplace.*

Gynics, male or female, tend to be insecure wall flowers at a party. They greatly appreciate the andric who comes up to them and introduces themselves. Gynics are the ones who would rather die than do public speaking. Talk about the epitome of insecurity. Public speaking is number one on their list. They smile readily, and this encourages the andric to lead the conversation. Gynics are good listeners. That's good, for the andric needs an audience.

Gynics are highly security oriented. They want the same paycheck each month, with set insurance, retirement (especially), and other benefits spelled out in great detail. Sell them additional insurance? Don't bother to ask. They have already called their agent years ago. They want the security of knowing that they (and their families) are covered – in case – you know – the "unknown" should creep into their lives. Disability income, car, fire, theft, children's college, flood, you name it. They are covered. They are cautious. With everything. They always set the home security system. The andric would say of them that they wear both a belt and suspenders. They are the "what if" people in a meeting in which the andric is saying "full speed ahead".

> *Never spring a new idea on a gynic or expect an instant decision.*

Never spring a new idea on a gynic and expect an instant decision. They need to "think about it". And they really do. They evaluate the pros and cons of every step before committing to a comfortable, non-emotional decision. They are very logical about their decisions. If there are 4 reasons to do, and 5 reasons to not do, then not do wins. They make endless lists, and generally follow them to the letter. Andrics make lists so that they can forget the items and go on to something more exciting.

I evaluated the andric snap-decision and gynic thought-out information in determining how to present dental treatment plans to patients. The same concept of androgynic decision making applies to any sales encounter. Andrics are more apt to want fixed bridges to replace teeth. These are appliances that are cemented to the remaining natural teeth. Andrics would rather have it placed and forget about it. Gynics are more inclined to look at the process. Fixed bridges require cutting down sometimes perfectly healthy teeth. Removable bridges do not require doing anything to surrounding teeth, but they have to be removed after each meal and rinsed off. Gynics consider that a small price to pay to save cutting down healthy teeth. Andrics don't want to be bothered with babysitting removable appliances. Gynics argue that they have to take their glasses off when going to bed anyway, so it is no big deal to remove a dental appliance. Who is right? Depends upon whether you are andric or gynic, that's all. If you know whether a person is andric or gynic, it is easier to lead them to a decision that they can live with for years to come. Present both cases, but lean toward the one they are most apt to find acceptable, then they do not feel guilty for their decision.

Andrics feel secure to make deals on a handshake. Gynics want a three page contract to get the newspaper delivered. And speaking of contracts, who writes most of the contracts? Lawyers. Almost all lawyers are gynics. They can sit at a desk and read past suits for three years and take their degree. Andrics can't sit anywhere for very long without going nuts. Lawyers are negotiators. Everything is to be done by the book – or books. They search for inaccuracies, for inconsistencies. They search. Sticklers for detail.

Courts are full of protocol. The way things are to be done. All rise. Please be seated. Black robes every time. Every time. Gynic lawyers love that type of security. They always know where they stand. It has been written, judged, notarized and cast in stone.

But! Who do lawyers *not* want on a jury? Andrics. Andrics cut through the subterfuge and make their decision based on the overall situation. Guilty or not guilty. Period. Gynic jurors can be shown 5 to 4 reasons for doubt, and will vote not guilty just because of their 5-4 internal decision. They are not secure with a decision unless they can count their reasons. Gynic lawyers can stir up confusion in gynic jurors with intimidation and lots of "facts". Andrics evaluate facts as to whether or not they are really facts, or just more subterfuge. They are apt to be elected jury foreman because they exude security, and will move things along faster than a confused gynic. On top of this, one has to consider that lawyers do not like to have highly educated people on the jury. A highly educated lawyer can easily sway a less educated, intimidated, gynic juror into seeing the step by step logic of his case. They like to schmooze the jury.

Unless they are female. Over the past three decades, many women have moved into jobs and professions formerly occupied by males. Law is one of them. Females in a formerly male dominant profession role are generally andric. Watch a male lawyer and you will see organization in action. Watch a female attorney and you will see a predator. Male gynic lawyers are pleased to negotiate and reach a 'happy medium' more often, whereas the female lawyer wants a total win, and the blood of her opponent on the floor.

Security is something andrics do not think about, it just is. I saw a real example of security oriented decisions once when we had an emergency situation in my office. We had a patient flown in in a med-vac jet. Her grandmother had read my book a week before. Grand daughter had had her teeth cleaned, and over the period of the next three days gone into a totally non-responsive coma.

"Could this mercury release from cleaning the amalgam fillings be responsible? The doctors here give her less than 48 hours to live."

Sure. Mercury does many bad things that get overlooked, but here was one that perhaps did not need to be relegated to the more-often-than-you-would-think category called "cause of death – unknown".

Their church raised the money for the jet in just a few hours. The next day she was in our office. I didn't know it at the time, but my four gynic dentists were panicked over which one I would assign to this case. They were coming from a place of insecurity. She had a good chance of dying any second. Certainly she would if nothing were done. What if something were done, though? Could she make it? Knowing the fear and trepidation a gynic dentist not accustomed to working in life-death situations would feel, I knew I was the only one willing to gamble on her dying in my hands. Actually the thought only briefly fleeted by. I may be only about a +2 andric, but I knew she had only one chance, if, in fact, the cleaning of fillings and release of additional mercury vapor was pushing her over the edge. There was no assurance that the cleaning was the problem, but, to me, this was no time for discussion.

I quickly assembled a team of physician, acupressurist, IV nurse, assistant I would not have to speak to (she could read my thoughts) and three other key personnel. The last person I spoke to was her mother.

"You know what can happen in there?" I queried her mother,

referring to the Bubble Operatory (a totally protective bubble shaped enclosure – looking like a giant pumpkin – with its own air filter system, laminar air flow, circular walls to aid stagnation of mercury laden air flow, negative ion generators to remove bacteria and mercury vapor, a Faraday Cage covering the room to reduce any electrical interference frequencies from radio, TV and the hundreds of radiant energies that bombard us daily and could affect brain function as highly charged electrical fillings were removed. As a side personal note – only an andric would waste that much money building a 'that' safe environment. This is not based on insecurity, but a desire to build a non-contaminating environment. This was for "now safety", not future "what if". Only a gynic judge would destroy it reasoning that its safety features implied that mercury was poisonous, therefore damaging to the reputation of the patent owners of amalgam. The American Dental Association.)

"Yes," Mother answered. "She could come out feet first. I'm prepared."

"Where do you want to be?"

"Right by your side."

"Why?"

"Because if she dies, <u>you</u> are going to need my help."

Talk about secure. She was the epitome.

During that procedure, we violated every principle I preach today. There was no way we could use a rubber dam on a person in an uncontrollable, potentially seizure creating coma, no time to consider electrical currents that could trigger the seizure, no time to check blood for compatibility to dental materials, no time to worry about crossing the mid-line. Talk about uncharted waters at night. No planning could be anticipated...just react and adjust instantly to whatever situation occurred.

My only worry was that she would live long enough to get the procedure started. My MD cohort had a bunch of syringes close to the IV port ready for events I did not even want to think about, but I knew I could trust her decisions. She was gynic and willing to follow my lead, knowing better than I what could happen – either way. I knew that she had already considered every eventuality that could happen. Being equal and opposite, we had total confidence in each other's decisions. No questions would have to be asked.

In the third quadrant of amalgam removal, she began to move. She didn't like the drill. She was feeling pain. A good sign. I was using no anesthetic for two reasons. I didn't need any more toxicity than was already there, and, besides, she was in a coma. Deep anesthesia. As I finished the third quadrant, paying no attention to the form of cavity preparation, paying no attention to marginal adaptation, very little attention to the bite, I began to feel that there were times when life was more important than protocol. She had 3 children and a husband who all loved her. So did her mother – and grandmother.

There were lots of challenges, and my team faced them all admirably. Ten years later, she is alive. Taking care of her family, and recently got a degree in accounting. Most folks have forgotten the case, but even as I write this, my eyes are filled with tears. During the procedure, my andric characteristics faced each unknown with instant responses. My team responded in androgynic fashion, for I selected them with androgynic cooperation in mind. I wasn't aware that Mother was at my elbow, or that my team was even in the room. Things just were. Things were happening as they should. God was probably our co-pilot, too. Calm, cool and collected we all were at the time. But today? No, my andric sensitivities cannot even let me tell about the case. I choke up now, but did not then. When it counted. My security paid off.

Andrics have feelings. Far too many.

I recently had a similar experience in which the physician was in control of the case. He was highly proficient, but insecure. He turned the

> *Andrics have feelings. Far too many.*

case away rather than face the possibility of having a death blemish on his record. By waiting, yes, perhaps the patient would die, "but not on my watch," was his comment.

"Why are you a doctor if death frightens you?" the andric in me asked.

"It's not death that bothers me, it's the lawyers."

A thousand miles away another doctor was waiting. He was not insecure. He took the chance. The patient is alive and very well.

Abrasive ✱✱✱ *Conciliatory*

Strong andrics are apt to be agitators. They stir the pot. Their gynic counterparts are apt to be conciliatory. They prefer status quo. They are into compromise and letting everybody win something. Andrics look at compromise as everybody lost something, and may not hesitate to tell you that.

You generally know where you stand with an andric. If they like you, they will do anything for you and speak in praising terms about you. If they do not like you, you will probably be aware of that, too. If they don't like you, they will be more apt to ignore you, but, in those cases, any attention you get from them, you may wish could have been avoided. If gynics don't like you, they are more apt to tell you where to go in such a way that you look forward to the trip.

In discussions with an andric it is likely to be "my way or the highway". Unless! If you can show an andric that there is really a better way, they may embrace your idea so fast that it makes your head spin. "Hey, you are right. Let's do it your way." It could be another forceful andric that points out the original error, or a gynic that points out the logic of the decision to call it an error, but either way it does not matter

> *In discussions with an andric, it is likely to be "my way or the highway". Unless!*

to the original andric. If this is better, let's do it – preferably now! Next problem?

Gynics are conciliatory. They understand that not everyone agrees on everything, and their goal is to find middle ground that everyone can tolerate. Maybe not be happy with, but no more name-calling, threats and yelling. Gynics have the time to listen. Or maybe they take the time to listen. They look for the good in every person or situation. Compromise is their mantra. Negotiation is their strong suit. However, if one side wants 10 and the other side wants 20, they feel that 15 represents an ideal goal. Andrics don't. They look for the original 10 or 20, with a possible 10% variation.

> *Gynics are conciliatory. Their goal is to find middle ground.*

Henry Higgins was portrayed as an andric. In his monologue in "My Fair Lady," he comments on compromise. "Form a plan and you will find she has something else in mind, so that rather than do either, you do something else that neither likes at all." That's an andric point of view on the subject of compromise.

Gynics do not raise their voices, if at all possible. To a gynic shouting is considered a loss of self control. To an andric, he's just voicing his opinion.

Active ✦✦✦ Passive

Two buzzards were sitting on a leafless tree on a very barren desert. One says to the other, "Patience my eye, I'm going to kill something." Surely that was the voice of an andric buzzard.

Animals are andric and gynic too, by the way. Sometimes humans put a male and female animal together for "breeding purposes". But occasionally the animals know innately that there is not a good endocrine match, and they won't have anything to do with each other. They know better than the human-calculated lineage charts what a good match is and isn't.

Patience is not in the andric's vocabulary, unless there is some *really big* reason for it. Like deep sea fishing for that 500 pound Marlin. But sitting in a boat on the local lake drowning worms – forget it.

> *Patience is not in the andric's vocabulary, unless there is some really big reason for it.*

Andrics have to have on-the-move jobs. They were that way in school, even in grade school. "Johnny, why don't you stay in your seat and behave like your brother Billy does?" Because Johnny has all this mini-testosterone encouraging his curiosity to explore and move out into life. Billy has all this estrogen telling him to remember what the teacher is saying because there will be a test, and he wants to get an A. Billy enjoys the family praise he gets for bringing home A's. The andric doesn't care so much about grades as he does about learning something he can DO. Something useful.

Who turns out to be the high school dropout? The andric. Johnny. Who earns the most PhD's? Gynics. Billy – (later turned Bill, then William). Who makes the most money? Andrics have a tendency to climb the ladders of business where 'no man has trod before'. They are risk takers. They may go broke a few times (aww, so what, it's only money) then hit on something that makes them wealthy. "How wealthy are you, Johnny?"

> Who turns out to be the high school dropout?

"I don't know. Ask my accountant. I've got a few grand here, a few there, own a few buildings, and this manufacturing plant whose taxes support the whole government for a few hours each year."

He probably leads a flamboyant lifestyle, drives a really nice car, dresses well, as long as color and pattern don't matter, and is a multimillionaire when he dies burned out in his forties – with or without a will depending upon the persistence of his chief accountant.

William (still his brother) is a strong hypothyroid gynic who 'has the first dollar he ever earned' framed in his office. The rest of the money from his paper route went into savings, and eventually into stocks and bonds of large stable blue chip companies. He has a master's degree, and perhaps even a doctorate in finance. His skills have gotten him elected president of the bank, president of the chamber of commerce, on the board of several non-profit organizations, and everybody loves him.

Everyone loves the gynic. They are the proverbial "nice guys". They never step on anyone's toes – or at least they will pad their shoes first. Andrics make what they consider the right decision and go for it without too much concern for other people's feelings. Feelings? What's that? It's the right decision. We'll come back to feelings later.

> Everyone loves the gynic. They are the proverbial "nice guys".

Gynics are masters at solving toe stomping situations. My father was gynic. Everyone loved him. He would make Will Rogers look like a hit man. Father loved to wander around my office talking to patients. He rarely introduced himself, just wandered up to people and engaged them in conversation about why they were there, how they got sick, how it affected them. He was truly interested in people and it showed. Dense white hair.

Once I found him chatting with a lady, and I knew he did not know who she was.

"Father, this is Mr. Celebrity's wife, Mrs. Celebrity."

"Oh, yes, well, I'm happy to meet you. I met your husband and have the greatest admiration for him. I know you must be proud of him. He has done so much for humanity."

"I am Ms. Maiden Name," she replied. "I happen to be Mr. Celebrity's wife, but I am a person unto myself, not just a Mrs."

Is she andric? Wow! 4 plus. I was really embarrassed for Father, but gynics can turn an event – if they are 4 plus – opposite and equal to the situation.

Father grinned and leaned toward her as if to say something in confidence.

"I'll bet you didn't talk about him that way <u>before</u> you were married," he said, with his winning smile. She broke into laughter, for andrics *can* be human – especially when defeated by a great negotiator gynic.

Andric

Nice guys get elected. They are the presidents of organizations, shapers of policy, the men up front in the three piece suits. The only way an andric becomes president is if he *owns* the company. Let's look at political presidents of our country. Or any country for that matter. Gynics. Nice guys. They have lots of support teams behind them. They share decisions. They work for compromise that will make 51% of the people happy and only 49% sad. That's what it takes to win an election. Right and wrong are not the key issues. Compromise is the word of the day. Every day. They have lots of committees and work well with them. We have had only one andric US president. Who was that? Most people miss that guess. It was Teddy Roosevelt – creator of the Rough Riders. He spoke softly but carried a big stick. Must have had a little bit of gynic in there for the speak softly part.

Same in the military. What are the generals? Gynics. Lincoln once appointed a nice guy that everyone liked and admired to lead a particularly critical attack. When the biggest battle of his career came up, he hesitated to attack for two days. The results of his hesitation caused many unnecessary deaths on both sides, and the loss

> *What are the generals? Gynics.*

of that battle, but he just couldn't bring himself to make the decision to go forward due to his own insecurity. What if he lost? His hesitation created the loss he was worried about.

Andric generals do occur once in a while. Remember Patton? Once Bradley called him to tell him *not* to attack a town. According to an extensive evaluation by the decision makers, Patton was outnumbered, under staffed, did not have enough fire power, and, logically, would lose the battle if they attacked. Patton knew his men, and infiltrated their spirits with his desire to win. Patton wired Bradley back a

Andric

typically andric sarcastic, "Have already taken the city. Should I give it back?" As you may remember, it was these kinds of quick decisions that got Patton 5 stars as well as trouble with his gynic superiors. He also said the Communists are going to stab us in the back. We have to stop them now. There was not enough hard evidence for the gynic politicians. He was right though, wasn't he? But he got fired for his beliefs.

Vacations

Vacations? To a gynic this means lengthy planning. A gynic retired air force colonel friend of mine recently gave me a 4 page itinerary for his Thanksgiving Holiday vacation trip. It included starting time, miles to destination, estimated gasoline refill locations, an elaborate Thanksgiving Day lunch menu captured off the internet, his and her choices of what they were going to order to eat, time for walking around town, time of the football game, and that was just the first page.

I have to remember that he had commandeered the largest air invasion in Viet Nam with well over one hundred huge aircraft timed to the second for take off, how many pounds of ordinance to carry, calculations of how many pounds of fuel to carry (none of this andric "fill 'er up"), fire power, coordinates of the targets, and how to come home without running into each other or running out of fuel. Magnificent feat. (I would hate to see what an andric would do with that task.) Now, that Thanksgiving Day vacation to him was a wonderful, relaxing event. Everything was pre-planned. Plan your work, and work your plan. First things first. These are comforting words to gynics.

Those same words are ulcer-producing to andrics. To have to conform to a schedule that omitted time for spontaneous creative ideas that must be written down instantly or lost forever would be great pressure to an andric. Vacation is a word yet to be understood by an andric.

Vacation to an andric means diversion. Go in another direction, but on the same latitude. Vacation means time to recharge your creativity batteries. Find new stimulations that allow you to think new thoughts. Rest the body? Yeah, to a certain extent, but a few hours will take care of that requirement.

> *Vacation to an andric means diversion.*

Gynics have multiple interests also. But unlike andrics, a

vacation to them can be to enjoy vicarious experiences through reading. They have colorful imaginations that can implant them into a novel such that they feel they have actually experienced the situations personally. They were there. They always have a stash of books that need to be read. Another one they want to read. They want to learn more about business by reading what other people have written who actually developed new concepts. Andrics want to invent things themselves, even though they can see that the gynic who learns from other's experiences through reading, experiences far less failure. Gynics like "vacation time" to catch up on their reading. This recharges their batteries. They take copious notes and highlight their books. Andrics highlight theirs, too, but that is so that when they re-read the book, they don't have to re-read the whole thing. Just the salient points.

Watch TV. It's all there. Just different interpretations applied by the andric viewer from the ideal vacation created by the gynic ad writer and gynic underwriter. Looks good to the gynic writers. Of course. They wrote the ads for themselves.

Picture a TV ad of someone wasting away in a hammock between two palm trees while reading War and Peace as a huge cruise ship awaits them in the background. Vacationers sit by a stagnant pool with a tinted blue bottom containing temperature controlled chlorine scented water, with bathing suit clad waitresses supplying perfect cocktails. Or, the counter opposite, parents smiling jubilantly at their screaming toddlers while they pee in that chlorine protected pool and run on the beach disrupting Frisbee enthusiasts who are trying to avoid the horses galloping along in the sand messing up sand castles that other kids made in an effort to protect the beach from invasion, or to cover up Dad with sand. Does this appeal to the andric or the gynic? Obviously the andric is turned off. Vacation advertisers should remember that andrics have money to spend on vacations, too. But you presented nothing that appeals to an andric. The spouse may be interested, but that kind of monetary investment must have something to satisfy both the andric and gynic.

Ten and twelve hour days for months on end, grabbing a handful of nuts for lunch, taking "stuff" home to work on at night and weekends...this can wear on an andric. He does need vacation time to recharge his batteries. But the batteries are <u>not recharged</u> by sticking him in a re-charger that sits on a ship overnight. Sitting on a beach watching water try to wear away a rock is not andric relaxation. Sitting *anywhere* does not recharge an andric. He requires *Diversion*. He recharges best while doing. Doing something that is unique. Different. In a different setting – a different town, country. Something that does not remind him of home and the things that are not getting done. Something intellectually stimulating, and not too vigorous physically.

Reading a book? Maybe on a topic that relates to his business from a different angle. But it better move. What's the point? Cruise ship? Yeah, sure. Unless it makes frequent stops at places of interest to that particular andric. Visits to Disney World with lots of different themes are not too bad. Las Vegas with many shows to choose from is not bad, but the gambling is not apt to be attractive. Andrics like to gamble on themselves, but not where the odds are known to be stacked against them. Get rich quick schemes are apt to fall on deaf andric ears.

A vacation to an andric who is forced by his business passion to scarf down food between projects, may actually include enjoying an extended dinner with super service, good wine that has been carefully discussed and selected and a tasteful cuisine. Maybe even ethnic cuisine. <u>Something different is recharging</u>. Something to challenge thinking as well as taste buds.

Believe it or not "shopping" in other cities is often of interest to andrics, as long as they can move from one place to another without dawdling. Unless it is to stop for a moment of "impulse buying". They like lots of new visual stimulation that does not require interaction. This is "restful", because it takes the brain from the known and semi-routine into the unknown. An andric's favorite haunt.

I know, the spouse is going to be "vacationed" by the equal and opposite desires, so therein lies one of life's mysteries of how can we compromise and still both have fun? Your call. That is what equal and opposites are all about. That's the real challenge to the advertisers. Develop diversion vacations that offer satisfaction to both the andric and gynic simultaneously.

In summary, andrics invented the on-off switch. Gynics invented the dimmer switch.

> *Andrics invented the on-off switch. Gynics invented the dimmer switch.*

Creativity ✲✲✲ *Organization*

Creativity and organization skills are at opposite ends of the same scale. The more andric a person, the more creative he may be, but the less organized. The more organized a person, the more he values status quo. Governmental regulatory agencies are full of status quo gynics who spend their lives trying to stifle the creativity of andrics who want change.

A really creative andric's desk looks like a terrorist training camp. "Stuff" is littered all over the place. Stacks of papers are straight in the first layer, then at an angle in the next layer, then upside down, anything to separate them, yet keep them in the same general area. Amazingly, they can still find things. The best example of this I have ever seen was in the movie "The First Week in October" in which Walter Mathau was playing the roll of a supreme court justice.

> *A really creative andric's desk looks like a terrorist training camp.*

He was in deep discussion with another justice when a court page came in with an intense expression on his face. Mathau stopped, glared at him and yelled,

"What?"

"The Chief wants the somebody vs somebody brief and says that you have it."

"On the table," Mathau retorts and returns to the conversation.

The page stares at the table, piled three feet high with briefs that look absolutely identical. He freezes. After a while Mathau notices that he is immobilized in front of the table and yells,

"What now?"

The page quivers and says, "Which one?"

Mathau mumbles an oath under his breath, walks over to the table and thrusts his hand into the middle of the stack, pulling out one brief. He hands it to the page without even looking at it and returns to his conversation. The page looks at the brief dumbfounded, for it is the right document. He hesitates for a moment, then when Mathau turns toward him again, he rushes for the door.

Recognizing the pattern and comparing it to my own desk, I laughed heartily at the scene in the theater. Then I noticed a bunch of gynics glaring at me for being disruptive during a scene that made absolutely no sense to them at all.

I thought judges were supposed to be gynic. They really are, but this is a good example of andric behavior. They really do know where things are in their messes, at least *most* of the time. For the other times, there are extremely valuable, competent, well organized, much appreciated, everything-has-a-place, gynic secretaries.

Gynic

Sometimes andrics have good intentions. They are not blind to their shortcomings, and often try to turn over a new leaf. I once bought two books called, "File, don't pile." Lost both of them on my desk. Great intentions, but andricity won out.

Andrics love change. Let's drive home a different way. Let's go a different route, even if it is longer, just to do something different. Something along the new way might ignite their creativity. It was probably an andric that had to wash dishes and sat down and invented the automatic dishwasher. He went on to something else while the gynic came along and patented it.

Andric

Andric's creativity comes from internal inspiration. It comes in flashes and lasts about that long. They cannot plan it in advance. That is why *andrics frequently interrupt conversations*. Inspiration came in a flash, and if they don't say what they are thinking at that moment, the creative comment will disappear from memory, never to reappear again.

Andrics can make great advertising people, if the great idea hits them before the deadline. They cannot create on command. Gynics are more dependable at logically figuring out what should work, even if at a moderate level of creativity, but they will have the ad organized and ready before the deadline every time.

Gynics have a place for everything, and everything in its place. That's organization. It required planning to invent, and planning to maintain. They also like to memorize. They are good in lodges or clubs that have a ritual. Ritual is highly respected and desired. Even at home. Breakfast at the same time each day, same for lunch and dinner. Grandma's for Sunday lunch. Every Sunday. Don't park in their space at work, or you will find that they are not always calm, cool and collected. They respect territory. Especially their own. Gynics are great meal planners for restaurants – make super chefs whose soup always tastes exactly the same. You can always count on it. Great flavor. Their creativity is spent in looking for ways to tweak long term proven tedious tasks. Not redesign, just tweak. They rely on carefully measured recipes. Andrics like to add a bit of this, a dash of that, a handful of something new, and each time their culinary achievement tastes different.

Gynic

Gynics excel at chess, bridge, or games that require thinking ahead and planning skills. They are accomplished with 500 piece puzzles and board games. Andrics have another opinion of *bored* games. This morning I saw a tax service ad. It demonstrated a bizillion puzzle pieces on the floor. The gynic-looking tax accountant was saying, "I love putting together these puzzles." The end frame showed putting the last piece into the puzzle to complete it. He looked so happy. He was. Andrics are also happy to pay a good price to make gynic accountants happy. Gynics are apt to stay at one job for one company for many years. They are fiercely loyal.

Fast Food *** Dining

Gynic

Andric

During the work week, fast foods and fast service are at a premium for andrics. They would just as soon go to a restaurant and ask the valet parking attendant to leave the car's engine running. Fast foods and fast service are desirable. If they have been to this restaurant before, they probably have their favorite selection and want to get things rolling – now! They are irritated by the waiter who drops off menus and waltzes off with a comment about I'll be back later to take your drink orders. If they give the waiter a drink order, they become even more irritated when the waiter disappears for another eternity – still not having taken the food order.

Having known before leaving for the restaurant what they want to eat, andrics are further irritated when the waiter insists on telling about the fish specials (specials are almost always fish, because if it isn't sold today, the restaurant has to throw it out tonight. It is almost spoiled already.). By the end of the meal, andrics are ready to get on with life, and drum their fingers waiting for the check. They may have wallet in hand when the waiter sneaks up during conversation, drops the check in a padded folder, and, looking at some far away destination, mumbles something about coming back for this *whenever you are ready*. Andrics are always ready. Andrics have a tendency to take all of this under consideration when figuring the tip – and when deciding whether to return to this restaurant or not.

Andrics are generally in a hurry. That's why they like buffets. They are fast and offer a wide variety of interesting items they can mix to their own creative satisfaction. Instant gratification, and back on the road again. Gynics prefer to be served. They like lengthy menus to peruse.

Gynics like to read each item on the menu to see if anything has changed since last time they were there, or to see what particularly appeals to them at this time. They listen carefully to the specials and compare them with the menu items. They savor each bite, and chew for all the flavor available in this culinary experience. (Andrics tend to bite the food a few times to cripple it, then swallow with a big slug of water to wash it down. Efficiency personified.)

> *Gynics like to read each item on the menu ... They savor each bite and chew for all the flavor available in this culinary experience.*

> *Andrics tend to bite the food a few times to cripple it, then swallow with a big slug of water to wash it down.*

Wine selection in itself can be a source of pleasure for the gynic, just mentally imagining the taste of each wine with each bite of food before they have ordered either their wine or their main course. Their food selection is apt to differ each time they visit the restaurant, and they expect foods to provide a new gustatory experience with each meal. Discussions with the waiters may include how many types of lettuce are in the salad, what is in the sauce, are the breads made here, or purchased from a bakery – lots of things that prepare their taste buds for a super experience. They are apt to comment on the "presentation" of the foods on the plate. They are not apt to have ulcers.

Andrics are happy to carry foods around with them at parties – or anywhere else, for that matter. Eating standing up is OK. If they are eating alone, they may take a small plate, put some munchables on it, and wander around the house. They may look out the window, read a small section of the paper, or just pace. Anything is better than sitting alone at a table. This is not too great for digestion, but they are not aware of that. Gynics prefer to sit down while eating.

Eating what? From the blood chemistry prospective, andrics do well on lots of meat. Gynics do not. Gynics feel bloated after eating a large steak. Why? They do not manufacture adequate enzymes for the task. Andrics require far more meat – like 200 to 300 percent more – to keep an andric's Total Protein level close to 7 grams percent. (The optimum level – if the albumin is at 4.6 G%). Gynics may be able to maintain 7 grams with as little as 2 ounces of meat daily. They can even skip a day and still do well. Andrics lose their energy if they miss a day of protein. Here I refer to animal protein. Vegetable protein is a different third dimensional shape from animal protein, and does not do the same thing in digestion.

Gynics can become vegetarians and function very well. Andrics feel a drop in energy within one or two days of abstaining from animal protein. Simple reason. Gynics do not produce as much hydrochloric acid and pancreatic enzymes into the stomach as andrics. This explains many dinner-time arguments about what is the best diet. Actually both partners are right. Just about different people. Themselves. Your self is the only real reference point you have. If you eat something and it "disagrees" with you, it is probably not on your

> *Andrics feel a drop in energy within one or two days of abstaining from animal protein.*

> *Gynics can become vegetarians and function very well.*

ancestral diet, and it is OK to avoid it – if it does not damage your body.

How would you know if your habits are damaging your body? Your chemistry knows. Can a vegetarian overdo avoiding protein? Some do. If a vegetarian's blood serum gets low on protein, in order to survive, his/her body will start breaking down already established self-protein for survival. They start losing muscle mass. It may take months or even years to get to this point, but when it does, it is easy to spot in the blood chemistry. They have a *high* Total Protein level. High? How can this be? I thought you said deficient. Yes, high, because the blood is now saturated with "self" body protein in an effort to survive the deficit.

I have been told more than once how this concept violates some religions and have been called many – actually just a few – names for my opinions. In reality, this is not an opinion. Just a report of facts of what is found in the blood chemistry. My job is to inform. I allow people to do what they want with the information I provide. No judgments.

What if these high Total Protein vegetarians decide to start eating protein? This creates a bit of a problem, for vegetarians cannot just start eating high volumes of meat overnight. The digestive tract has to reorganize digestive enzymes and bacteria in order to accommodate the change. They may have to get into dental revision procedures slowly, for we encourage a high animal protein diet prior to surgical removal of root canals, cleaning of cavitations and anything else that results in bleeding that requires healing. Without animal protein, these people experience lengthy and painful healing with lots of swelling and bruising. As might be expected, andric vegetarians will suffer more with slow healing than gynics.

If vegetarians increase their dietary protein intake, the blood Total Protein level drops precipitously within a day or two. *Drops?* What kind of sense does that make? Plenty, if you know how blood operates. At first, the blood protein level was high with self-donated protein to *compensate* for lack of protein intake in the diet. As soon as protein of the right third dimensional match appears in the diet, the body stops digesting itself, and the true serum Total Protein level appears. I have seen Total Protein levels in the blood drop from 7.8 grams or more to 6.2 or below in 4 or 5 days after vegetarians begin to consume protein. It generally requires assistance in the form of supplementation to teach the body how to digest protein again, for if a person has been a vegetarian for more than a month, the body loses it ability to digest proteins properly. Use it or lose it concept.

Gynics make great chefs. Andrics make great cooks.

Gynic

Gynics pay attention to every detail, and make sure presentation is color coordinated with the plates, table cloths, napkins, etc. Their end product flavors are generally a blend of many herbs and spices such that you cannot identify the components. Their foods present a truly unique taste experience.

Andrics like to grill steaks outside, prepare flaming desserts, anything flamboyant, but they are not much on garnishments. They are Johnnie-One-Notes in the kitchen. You will probably get a plate and silverware in addition to your steak, but the meal may

Andric

be short of garnish, salad, soup and appetizers. You won't be disappointed, for the flavor of the food you get will make a statement. One clear and tasty statement. Not a blend.

Andrics like spices they can identify. Cinnamon rolls, cumin, nutmeg, salt, pepper, tabasco. Gynics prefer blends that present a new palatal sensation like a blended perfume tempts the aroma sensations. Like a water color picture where it is difficult to differentiate one hue from another.

Gynics prefer salads, andrics prefer blonds.

Call for the Psychologist

Why? Because he/she is not behaving properly. What that really means is that some andric/gynic is not behaving the way his/her gynic/andric judge is calling it. Who is really right/wrong? Probably neither, just being.

Double talk? Close to it, because double talk is the world that andric/gynic mates live in. The farther apart from the ideal line they are, the more differences they perceive in the other partner. If it's different, then, obviously, it is wrong.

> *Statistically, the psychologist is going to be right 50% of the time and wrong 50% of the time.*

Psychology is probably one of the most frustrating areas in which to work. Statistically, the psychologist is going to be right 50% of the time, and wrong 50% of the time. Why? Because almost all psychologists are gynics. If they are working with couples, they are apt to be working with one andric and one gynic. That's where their 50% success / failure rate comes from. Their assessment of behavior is naturally going to be based on the idea that if you do not possess gynic behavior, then you are possessed. A little easier to understand now, after reading the preceding part of this book?

Gynic psychologists, ministerial counselors, probation officers, etc., tend to tell an andric misbehaver to adopt gynic behavior in order to fit into society. Actually, into *their society of conformity*. That is like a scientist telling an electron to jump from one orbit to another. It can be done, but it requires a great deal of external energy.

Counselors would be far better able to mediate people if they had an understanding of the androgynic and other hormonal factors creating their client's behavior / misbehavior. Especially, how *their own endocrine balance* is active in helping them determine which party is the origin of the problems. A hypo-thyroid counselor immediately identifies the hyperthyroid client as the causative factor in blame assessment. A gynic counselor also blames (maybe subliminally) the andric client as the trouble maker. The hypo-posterior pituitary counselor may identify *both* parties as reprobates, and beyond help.

If psychologists could work within the framework of knowing that "there's a place for us" as the song goes, a place for all andrics, gynics, hypo and hyper glandular individuals, their success rate might increase. But that would require working within the mold of the *clients*, and disregarding the "gynic only" mold that most counselors are taught.

Understandably, copying a different type of behavior does *not* alter a person's blood chemistry. They will still require carbohydrate, protein and fat, and will still have adverse reactions to sugar, alcohol and caffeine. Nor is copy-catting very successful in long term behavior alteration. Biblically, Saul became Paul, but, although he changed his direction of occupation for the better, his methods of achieving goals did not change.

> *Copying a different type of behavior does not alter a person's blood chemistry.*

Identifying the root causes of behavior soon exposes the fact that behavior is the result of hormonal response to external stimuli, and not necessarily that a person is innately bad just because he is different from you. He looks at the world through a different lens. We all color our own lenses.

> *Behavior is the result of hormonal response to external stimuli.*

Counselors could benefit from knowing that andrics are good leaders. Poor followers. They can rile people up for the battle, but when it is time to attack, it is the gynic that needs to pull out the compass and map to determine which direction the team should go. Both are necessary, but they require their own definition of space.

Counselors should know that gynic bearded males are generally dominated by strong andric females, AND, that both are happy in this relationship. They may pretend otherwise, but the gynic male does not really feel upstaged as much as he is acting. That is a condition reserved for andrics. The reserved gynic does not need to go through assertiveness training. That adds guilt and stress that can lead to feelings of inadequacy – something that needs no encouragement.

Gynic

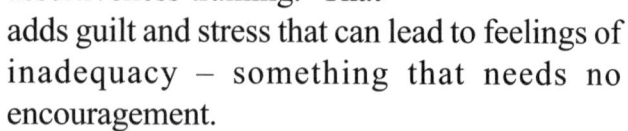

Andric

Both male and female andrics want to steer the boat. Put them at the tiller and let them stand up there with the wind and salt water in their face. They are not wired to sharing 50-50 in decision making, unless they really do not know which direction to go, then they honestly desire input. They will ask for it. A counselor would do well to say, "Give input graciously and do not point out all the mistakes that could have been avoided in the past if they had this attitude earlier in life."

Counselors should be aware of the andric male, andric female tussle. Watch out for this one. This is where "mediation" is sometimes recommended. One person in one room, the other in another room. Remember that Mother Nature does not like birth defects. Andric - andric crosses are more prone to produce abnormal offspring. Mother Nature wants to keep these people away from each other. You may be observing the results of this natural un-attraction. Andric male vs andric female do not just have sparks. They do not just rain on each other's parade. They throw gasoline. This *may not* be a situation that "counseling" can improve. It may really be hormonal. Consider letting them go their separate ways, rather than staying together and doing bodily injury to each other.

Andrics tend to exaggerate, but notable so, so that it does not become classified as lying. They will not say that the temperature was 42 when it was really 45; if they are cold, they will say that the temperature was 99 below zero.

Now for the big challenge for the counselor. After you have determined who is andric, gynic, hypo and hyper, something happens. Mid-life alterations. Like flip side. Total reversal. Well, maybe not total, but enough to change all the rules. Somewhere over the age 50 rainbow, andrics mellow and gynics become more aggressive. They both act like late bloomers. Body chemistry wise, it still takes the same hormones to balance them, just lesser dosages. But behavior changes. The two partners sort of recognize this change, but it is so subtle and welcome that neither is uncomfortable.

Can this become a problem? You know it. Nothing involving human interaction is ever smooth. Not as bad as a sex change, but there are similarities. Say two people marry, she is 28 and he is 42. That is a 14 year difference. If the endocrine patterns are equal and opposite, things will be fine. For about 10 years. Then the 52 year old male starts turning from gynic to andric, or the other way around, andric to gynic, and Woops!

What happened to the person she married? Metamorphosis. All of a sudden, they are not communicating like they used to. Their interests are not as compatible as before. The mother-in-law says, "I told you that you should not marry such an old man". Is he just getting old? Well, not at 52, but his focus has changed, and "age" is a handy cop out. Mid-life crisis. If they do work it out, adjust, and stay together, then, when *she* hits 50 or so, she undergoes a flip side change, and you repeat the same story again. Now you have to go through the equivalent of puberty all over again – for the third time.

Is it worth it? Your call. Should be easier this time, for you will be back on the same relative footing (although equal and opposite) to what brought you together in the first place.

Dress Codes

Andric males are apt to have one color of slacks. Black is a good neutral color, and it is easy to find shirts and jackets to go with black. Basic black is not just for women. They may also prefer to have one type of socks. They might be black too. They might have 2 dozen of them, all alike. Cuts down matching socks after the laundry. They got that way by being razed unmercifully by gynics who pointed out that their socks were close, but not mates.

Better yet, an andric male likes to have his gynic wife pick out his clothes. Buy them too. They do such a great job of matching things up and making the andric male look nice. Andrics like to look nice, they just don't have the patience to learn what looks nice, and how to mix and match. Now, there are those who get really interested in clothes. They are apt to go overboard and even get to the point of designing their own apparel.

Gynics are generally into current fashion, and pay rapt attention to texture, hue as well as color, harmonizing and contrasting colors, and all the intricacies of being dressed for success. They want their clothes properly pressed, and the linings of garments exactly the proper length so that they don't pull the external material into an unwanted wrinkle.

> *Gynics are generally into current fashion ... Gynics are apt to be neatness freaks.*

They are fashion plates even if only going to the grocery store. When they go to ultra restaurants, watch out. They will be stunning.

Gynics are apt to be neatness freaks. Andrics may pull up the covers on the bed, but are not apt to tuck them in – unless at the bottom where feet are getting cold. That is a reason – a purpose – therefore it affords extra attention. Gynic's homes, cabinets, drawers, kitchens, garages are apt to be very neat and orderly. Ever see a garage in which the outline of tools is carefully painted on the wall? That is neatness unfathomable to the andric mind.

Now, honesty is something you have to be careful with concerning andrics. Ladies, don't ask your andric husband what he thinks of your clothes selection unless you want a direct answer. He may not have noticed anything, and just pass it off by saying, "looks fine", or "looks great". But, if he doesn't like it, brother. Beware. You will get an honest answer with no holds barred. And not real vengeance. Just an honest assessment. Isn't that what you ask for?

Sports

Who's the good sport? Depends upon the sport. Andrics are not too much into sports, but when they are, it is generally an individual sport. In competition with themselves, if possible. They tend toward things like skiing, snowboarding, hiking or tennis, ping pong, the javelin throw, handball, where only one or two other people are involved. Solo is best. Golf wastes too much of an andric's time, although he may enjoy hitting a bucket of balls on the driving range. Gynics like golf, because it gives them time to talk to friends or business associates without as many interruptions as one finds in offices.

Gynics like team sports. They like doing things together. Hockey, basketball, football, volleyball. Get together with the fellows and have a good physical time on a group basis. On a more individual basis they enjoy bridge and chess games that require strategic planning and concentration.

Gynic

Gynic males sometimes have trouble with their masculinity. They watch andrics walking around fussing about things, and feel that they are really in control. To feel more masculine, some gynics may take up boxing. That is a controlled sport. No one is going to get killed – you do wear protection – and besides, there are rules. It is quite physical and looks very masculine. The ultimate is football. Gynics are physically built for it. Heavy and muscular. Their weight is distributed fairly evenly. Andrics look at football games with 300 pound bruisers running into each at full speed, and think, "You could get hurt doing that". Gynics are more apt to think, "If I don't do it, it's a blot on my manhood." You will rarely find andrics on the gridiron or in a boxing ring trying to prove their manhood. It never crosses their minds. They will be in the cheering crowd and be quite supportive, even donate for a new stadium, but join the team? No way. Back to the badminton court. On to skiing.

In Sickness *** and *** In Health

Doctors would be better able to direct patient health activities if they were aware of the Androgynic Factors involved with disease susceptibility. Let's start with a simple one that directly involves estrogen and testosterone. The "pill". The birth control pill is a heavy dose of estrogen. When it first came out, some women noticed very little side-effect, others noticed a lot. Research was difficult, for the drug industry was trying to come out with a dose where one size fits all regardless of body weight. Or the Androgynic Factor.

> *Doctors would be better able to direct patient health activities if they were aware of the Androgynic Factors involved with disease susceptibility.*

Who do you suppose tolerates an extra hit of estrogen, and who doesn't? The andric female already has an overdose of testosterone, so a bit of estrogen better balances her blood chemistry and emotional state. Not quite so abrasive, and the phosphorus level may improve slightly. Birth control pills were easily accepted by andric female endocrine systems. Gynics already have an overdose of estrogen, so additional just makes them more weepy, more emotionally unstable, and drops their phosphorus level so that they are more susceptible to picking up major or minor diseases.

As far as weight is concerned, gynics are more apt to be overweight than andrics. Not a hundred percenter, but certainly greater than 70% true. This should be an item that is factored into the birth control pill equation as well.

Root canals produce different effects on the andric than the gynic. Again, this is a

> *Root canals produce different effects on the andric than the gynic.*

generalization based on a large population sample. Not just 5 people. Toxins are produced in root canal teeth that are some of the most powerful poisons on the planet. Just a few milligrams of molecules can create health problems, and molecules cannot be seen in a blood test – certainly not on an X-ray.

When hit with these toxins, andrics are apt to become more susceptible to heart attacks. Strong statement? Look at the thousands of cases that Dr. Weston Price performed when head of research for the American Dental Association. He was able to remove root canal teeth from people who had had heart attacks, implant them in rabbits, and reproduce the heart attack (as noted by the death and subsequent autopsy of the animal) in approximately 10 days. We are not talking about a few, but thousands of autopsy tests that, even today, are admired as superior research.

The causes of these heart attacks was originally discovered at Mayo's Clinic in the early 1910's by microbiologists and pathologists who were (by today's standards) the finest pathologists the world has ever seen. Eyeballs and interpretations based on experience are still the major key to successful diagnosis in pathology.

We must also factor in smoking, drinking caffeine containing beverages, alcohol and other lifestyle events — but, Hey! Those are the same factors that push the gynic over the edge. Gynics, however do not have to worry much about heart attacks. If they do have one, it is not apt to be fatal, and they can experience a rapid recovery, if put on the proper body chemistry regimen. Little chance of heart attack in your future Mr. or Mrs. Gynic. Your hormones are pointed toward cancer. Oh, brother. Thanks a lot.

Our reactions to these issues are usually based on our immortality complex. The fact is that double blind studies over the years have proved that none of us is going to get out of this life alive. The only choice we have is just how miserable are we going to be during the last years of our life, and how many of those years there are going to be.

Estrogen dominant tissues (the gynic) are more cancer prone, for added estrogen stimulates cell growth. If you have been diseased, then repair of those cells is desirable, and that, in turn, calls for estrogen. Controlled cell growth, with all the proper nutrients. Dr. Page used estrogen extensively – primarily on andrics. Diseased gynics usually require *small* doses of testosterone in order to produce the same degree of healing by controlling the amount of estrogen present. Excess estrogen in the gynic is apt to produce uncontrolled cell growth, which by another name is called cancer.

> *Estrogen dominant tissues (the gynic) are more cancer prone, for added estrogen stimulates cell growth.*

This one really irritates me. It doesn't have to happen. If you are female, you can increase your chances of breast cancer early in life. Just have a couple of "chrome crowns" put on your baby teeth. This provides a nickel mediated immune challenge. Later, have braces for a couple of years. This offers a second carcinogenic challenge to your immune system, but if you are young enough, your immune system can fight it off, too. Next fracture a cusp off of a tooth when you are in your early thirties. This leads to a root canal and ceramic crown fired over a *nickel* based crown, and Bingo! Your immune system says, "enough". It then succumbs to rapid cell division – and for some reason (unknown to me) picks on the female breast on the same side as the root canal. Every time? No, but over 90% of the time it will be "ipsolateral". Interesting that the microscopic pathology slides of root canal – nickel related breast cancer all look very much alike. Now, you too can be added to the ranks of breast cancer of undetermined origin. Oh yes, I forgot. That is, if you are gynic.

Sure, there are other factors as mentioned. Sugar, alcohol, caffeine play their role as well as other things. But! Dental materials in your mouth is one thing that you have some control over. If you are informed. Cancer does not occur because of one solitary item, but nickel and root canals have an out-of-proportion influence on malignant development. If you are gynic, argue the point. If you are andric, be informed and *do* something. Even if it is only, as Nancy Reagan says, "Just say no".

How can this situation be? Again, this is a really big challenge to our health profession. And another good question: why haven't I heard about this before? For some reason or another, dental magazines do not want to carry this information. No one does. Look at the potential liability.

Let's look at known science behind these statements. Nickel is the most carcinogenic (cancer producing) metal known to science. New information? No. Nickel as a carcinogen has been written up in the scientific literature for over 70 years. Is it worse than mercury I am noted for fighting? Well, mercury tends to kill cells, nickel does not. Nickel just makes the cells malignant. Which would you rather have? A dead cell or a malignant one? Your choice, for *you* determine what you allow your dentist to place in your body.

> *Nickel is the most carcinogenic metal known to science.*

Now let's look at your childhood. That "chrome crown" that you had placed on a baby tooth when you were 6 years old is a cutesy name for nickel. There is some chromium – and cobalt together in that crown, but the primary ingredient is nickel. By the way, chrome and cobalt are not carcinogenic. Unless they are mixed *together*. The combination of the two *is* carcinogenic. Alloyed together as in a chrome crown. This first exposure of nickel explains to your immune system that it is cancer producing, and it better watch out. Your immune system develops an onslaught against the nickel, but is *wounded* in the process.

Later, you get orthodontic braces. Many of the bands are made of nickel, and the arch wire and brackets are made of nickel. Your immune system is further wounded, but makes a valiant attempt to fight back.

Now comes the big event of your life. That nickel based crown with aluminum oxide (marketing people call it porcelain) fired onto it plus the root canal with extreme toxins, can push your immune system over the edge. Then, the combined cancer stimulating properties of the root canal and the nickel win out. Breast cancer. One can even predict what the microscopic evaluation will be. Hard to believe? I certainly did not believe it when I first discovered the connections. Any idea how many chrome crowns, orthodontic wires and root canals I had done? Do me a favor. Don't tell St. Peter.

> *The combined cancer stimulating properties of the root canal and the nickel win out. Breast cancer.*

Now, let's join the observation people. Look backwards. There are many people with root canals who do *not* have breast cancer. But! Look at the ones who *do have (or have had)* breast cancer. Number one, did they have dental exposures to nickel? Number two, did they have a root canal? Lifestyle evaluation including sugar, alcohol, caffeine and exercise, yes. And, I almost forgot. Are they gynic?

Andric females with the same dental history can develop breast cancer, but it is more likely to be localized. Most lumps and bumps are going to be benign, but even if they are malignant, it rarely metastasizes to the surrounding lymph nodes. Surgical lumpectomy may be all that is required, and radiation and chemotherapy are apt to supply more damage than good to the andric female as far as patient survival is concerned.

Controversial? You bet. But at this stage of my life, I really don't care if informing the public of true facts makes me controversial. You have a right to know these things. From these observations, you are welcome to make your own decision – however, make it an informed consent. But! How can you make a choice if you have only one view to evaluate? That's like a third world election in which only one person is running for office. If the dental shoe fits...why fight it? I think I now know why I fight it. Gynic surgeons and researchers are insecure if they accept a new view. Andric females will scream, why were we not told this? Hey! Scream! That may lead to action. Breast cancer is a condition that does not have to happen. My opinion.

Breast cancer is only one example of the many diseases available from "Cancer, Root Canals and Nickel Associates Inc.". There is no harm in becoming informed. No harm to you. Maybe to industry, but I am writing for you.

Who do you suppose develops ulcers? You got that one right. Andrics. What about colon problems? Digestive problems? More apt to be gynics, but I'm not sure why. Only an observation.

You might expect that andrics tend to run higher blood pressure than gynics, and that appears to be true. Especially if they have root canals. There is a high probability that high, uncontrollable blood pressure will come into range – without medication – if root canal teeth are removed properly. A whole other story there. Most are not removed properly, for the periodontal ligament must be removed as well as the tooth. High blood pressure is not to be equated to steam pressure. People do not have more energy due to having higher blood pressure.

> *Andrics tend to run higher blood pressure than gynics ... if they have root canals.*

Actually, either andrics or gynics can develop high blood pressure – if they are reacting to a root canal tooth. When all else has failed, removal of an offending root canal can substantially reduce high blood pressure within a few days –

even without medication. If, if, if. If the periodontal ligament is removed after the tooth is removed. If proper protection involving IV procedures and post operative ice packs, magnets – actually a whole slew of items – are employed during and after the surgery. I am not implying that the simple removal of a tooth will bring the blood pressure down any more than simply removing silver-mercury fillings will heal a person injured by mercury. Pulling the pin out of the balloon quickly after puncturing it will not put the balloon back together.

Perplexing Habits

I shall now explain the habits that have perplexed humanity since the exodus of the Sears and Roebuck catalogue, and the emergence of toilet paper.

Men and women have always argued the reasoning behind having the toilet paper feed over the top of the roll as contrasted with from underneath. The argument is actually based on married men and women generally being andric and gynic, not because they are male and female.

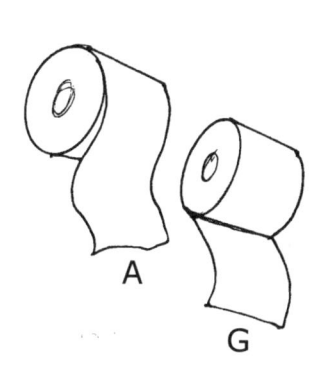

The answer to this irritation to cohabitation lies in the fact that andrics prefer top feed, and gynics prefer bottom feed. There is no right nor wrong. It is a matter of preference. That is why the argument persists. Each knows that they are right, and that is right. For them. There is no logic or science behind it, it just is.

And speaking of top feed vs bottom feed, andrics and gynics differ in their driving position. In a relaxed state, like driving on the Interstate between cities, the gynic's hands are on the bottom of the steering wheel, palms facing up. Andrics enjoy driving, but have a hard time experiencing this relaxed state. They drive with their hands, often just one hand, on the top of the steering wheel, palms facing down. Reason? Same as the toilet paper issue. It just is.

Driving the speed limit? That *is* smart – if the cops are around. Time to toe the line. Otherwise 8 miles an hour over the speed limit is reasonable. Andrics were the first to buy fuzz busters, but 8 miles over the speed limit is not always compatible with their hurried schedule. Their schedule does not always allow for red lights, traffic jams, the need to put gasoline in the car – some of those unforeseen, irritating interruptions.

Stop signs present different problems – and solutions – for andric and gynic drivers. Remember, I am talking about males and females both. This may sound like masculine behavior, but it is relative hyper testosterone in either sex.

The light turns yellow. The gynic tries to bring the car to a smooth stop very carefully calculating the deceleration increments necessary to come to a smooth, even stop.

Andric behavior? Pedal to the metal. There is still time to squeeze across the intersection before red appears. Especially if you close your eyes. There is some question about just how fast the speed of light really is. Red may travel relatively slower than yellow, allowing the andric more time to clear the intersection.

To an andric, road signs are there to control traffic. By definition, traffic involves more than one vehicle, so they adjust their behavior according to how many vehicles are present. To a gynic, signs are there because of a law. Laws are there to be obeyed. They are cast in stone.

Ask a gynic what S.T.O.P. stands for, and his answer might be "skid tires on pavement". An andric might reply "slow to observe police".

Gynics were elated when car computers came out with instant and long term gasoline mileage calculators. That saved them from parking at the pump with the same tilt, listening to the flow of gas into the tank so that the cut off point was at the same place, keeping very accurate records of mileage to the tenth, and having a calculator in the glove compartment all the time just for mileage calculation.

Andrics were not as concerned about mileage. Look on the sticker when you buy the car, and forget about it. The andric was happier with the mileage set button that tells him how many miles to the destination. Ten, nine, eight...that interests him more. That plus the time it takes to get there. That's practical.

Gynics read a lot. They especially like long books, so if they get enchanted with the book, the feeling will last a long time. They may enjoy reading War and Peace. Andrics read CliffsNotes, or the Reader's Digest condensed version. Better yet, have someone else read the condensed version, and highlight it for them.

> *Computers fascinate gynics and irritate andrics.*

Computers fascinate gynics and irritate andrics because they can't see anything but the screen. Andrics cannot verbally negotiate or discuss options when they do something wrong. Gynics know how to work backwards, use Norton Utilities, reverse the last change, all things that the andric has not taken the time to learn about. Easier to hire a gynic secretary who can fix everything the andric has messed up. Gynics learn that there is an endless stream of programs that will help them work out solutions logically. Andrics don't need that. A simple yes or no will do.

Directions. Who follows them? Who needs them? Gynics read the directions, *all* of them, prior to beginning the assembly process. Andrics do not feel the need to read directions unless forced by the situation to determine the starting point and end point. If there is a 20 page set of detailed directions, *and* a "Quick Start Guide", you know that the company has figured out that there are both andrics and gynics out there in the purchasing market. The andric may glance at the Quick Start – especially if there are lots of pictures and large print. Otherwise he lets his sense of adventure and astute powers of creativity take over. Right or wrong. Usually wrong. Eventually he may have to accede to the gynic for assistance. Or just let the project end up with the multiple other half-finished projects in the basement.

Now, for the major post-marital conflict. — What is the *proper* way to squeeze the tooth paste from the tube? There are extremely logical explanations for this, even from the andrics. But the real truth of the problem is that andrics squeeze from the middle and gynics carefully roll the tube from the bottom up. That's it. Not right or wrong. Not more or less efficient. What's right is what makes your hormones hum.

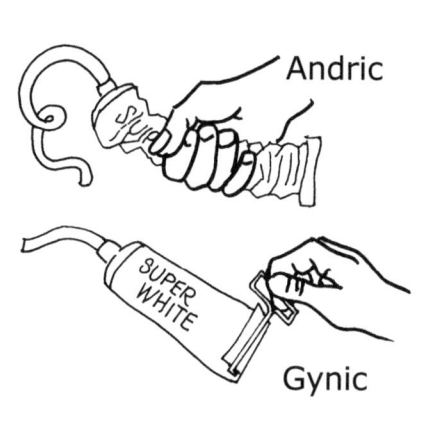

Smoking. Although not as popular as it was a few decades ago, the tobacco industry still holds a major niche in the stock market. Andrics prefer to smoke cigarettes. Why? This one is fairly obvious. It is fast and convenient to slip a cigarette out of its pack, light it, and you are on your way, talking while smoking. Contrast this with pipe smoking. Only a gynic would take the time to pull out a pipe, clean its bowl, pour in fresh tobacco from a pouch carried some obscure place on his person, compress the tobacco to just the right consistency that it is not too hard to suck air through it, yet enough to mix the aroma of one of many blends of tobacco such that he could get the maximum olfactory stimulation, keep relighting it if the puffs are a few seconds late to reignite embers from the last puff, then clean and store it after the aromatic and satisfying experience. Definitely a gynic pleasure. It would drive an andric up the wall just to have to relight a cigarette. When you are through with a cigarette, just give it a flip. No time-wasting task unless you have to look for an ashtray.

Let Me Entertain You

<u>Movie stars</u>, entertainment stars, well known or popular people I should say. I'm not sure why this one is, but it is obvious that this is the trend. Male movie stars — the big ones – are gynic. Female big movie stars are andric. Now that male - female combination makes for the most realistic movies, for andric males matched against andric females are not going to make the best actors to put across a point. Equal and opposite intensities are required for a movie to click with an audience. Take Rhett and Scarlett in "Gone with the Wind". Gable was one of the finest gynic actors that ever graced the screen. Scarlett was an equal and opposite 4+ andric. Close to Gable was John Wayne. Who didn't like the Duke? I remember once in the movie "The Cowboys", Wayne was killed. That had never happened – and should never happen to real heroes. The audience with no cue roared in disbelief. They were crushed, because *everyone loved John Wayne* and wanted him to live forever.

> Male movie stars — the big ones – are gynic.
> Female big movie stars are andric.

Burt Reynolds, Jimmy Stewart, Tom Cruise, Sean Connery, I like Ike, Harrison Ford, Elvis, Tom Selleck, Richard Burton, Charlton Heston, even Arnold is gynic.

What about andric male stars? Yeah, a few exist, but they are few and far between. Yul Brynner, George C. Scott who stood up against the Academy Award for his Non-yielding opinion. He *might* have been andric, but he certainly portrayed the andric role of Patton in the movie. One might think andric behavior in watching Schwarzenegger in any movie, Hannibal Lectur in "Silence of the Lambs", and Robert Shaw in "Jaws", but the cool, calculating, non-emotional behavior gives them away. They are all gynics. Andrics fuss about violent behavior, but are not often found actually doing it.

Females. Check out the andric stars Liz Taylor, Bette Midler, Joan Rivers, Rosie O'Donnell, Katharine Hepburn, Hillary. She is not a movie star, but most everyone knows who she is. Good example of 4+ andric in formerly gynic male domain.

I recently saw the movie "Paycheck". Andric-gynic behavior showed up in one part just like you would predict. Ben Affleck and his movie girl friend Uma Thurman are in the inner sanctum and could be raided by the bad guys at any moment. As an andric reaction, she picks up a huge lengthy wrench she has been hoarding for special occasions and says, "Aha! This is what I have been saving this for." She prepares to take a mighty swing and smash the electronic lock into eternity, the past, whatever, anyway, she is going to destroy it in one fell swoop. He stops her. Not physically, just says softly and gynically, "Wait a moment". In ten seconds, he disassembles the lock with a small Allen wrench, removes a critical electronic component and places a half dollar over the electronic connectors. This results in an electronic nervous breakdown of the complicated lock. This assures us that the bad guys will not be able to enter without strong force that just fracturing the lock might not have achieved.

Why do we enjoy cartoons? One reason is that the humor we relate to is often a reflection of our own Androgynic Factor. Ever cut out a cartoon from the newspaper and give it to someone you know? Like a spouse? Work associate, close friend? Hey! This is *you*. This is *us*. We relate to cartoons because those folks have the same problems that we do. The long running successful cartoons usually have a good match between andric and gynic. The most successful cartoons should be the ones that have exaggerated andric and gynic traits. They are like drawings called caricatures. In drawings, the artist takes a slight imperfection in the person he is drawing and exaggerates it. Big nose, big eyes, big ears, eyes too close together, huge moustache – exaggerate the obvious. That is what cartoonists do with the Androgynic Factor. Take the normal equal and opposite reactions and put them under a magnifying glass.

People can relate to those roles. Who is more gynic than good ole Charlie Brown? (Maybe Pogo.) Who is more andric than Charlie's co-star Lucy? (Maybe Granny in Beverly Hillbillies.) Perhaps competitors would be Mammy and Pappy Yocum from L'il Abner. Mammy smoked a pipe and single-handedly went into the cave to beat up the "It" about once a year. Could be considered andric behavior – exaggerated. Pappy was as equal and opposite a laid back person as she was a rabble rouser and defender of humanity. Now their kids. Abner, a real lovable gynic, married a gynic, and the cartoon died. Perhaps the cartoonists did too – extenuating circumstances, but it was Mammy who carried the script. Dagwood and Blondie are long term examples of an androgynic couple who stayed together more than 50 years. He is the andric bumble footed fellow who is constantly running headlong into the mailman. His clock never takes into account that there might be a red light that would throw off his planning by 30 seconds. Always late – not much, but late just the same. He takes each day as it comes, and she is very organized and logical. Even in the funny papers, those who are equal and opposite last.

Offense ✭✭✭ *Defense*

Andrics yell a lot. Maybe not so much in decibels, as in being vocal about their opinions, but they make themselves heard. Perhaps just short of threats and often with a slight humorous twist. They act like they are going to act. Gynics sit back and think about how to resolve the situation without the physical violence that is suggested by the andric. Andrics do not often get involved with the physical, but they sound very manly to the gynic and the gynic may eventually try to act out things that visually resemble "manhood moves".

"If you don't (fill in the blank), then I'm gonna (fill in the blank)." This might be the format of antagonism used by an andric. This may involve anything from "get out of that seat" to "leave my girl friend alone", and the result may range from bloody your nose to let the air out of your tires. Politicians may use andric threats like if you don't move your troops out, I'm a gonna cut off our trade agreement with you that will cost you bizillions of dollars. That actually smells of andric and gynic both. Maybe it represents committee action.

Gynics can be very clever in avoiding physical confrontation. My uncle was a gynic amongst several andric siblings. He was the youngest. Two strikes. Grandmother used to get a nickel's worth of candy sticks at the grocery store once a week. At that time it was a handfull. She divided it up among the 5 kids. The andrics scarfed their candy down in a couple of minutes while their gynic brother slowly licked his and savored each molecule of sweetness. As might be expected, the older siblings threatened, and if that didn't work, confiscated his candy.

Uncle did not have great stature at 46 pounds, but did have a calculating gynic mind. He devised a simple, but extremely effective defense even though outnumbered and verbally intimidated. When the candy was dispensed, he carefully licked every stick before engaging in the actual act of consuming his candy. When the other kids saw him contaminating his candy with oral cooties, they lost interest in "sharing" his booty anymore. Nothing physical, but highly effective visual negotiating skills that were probably the basis of his being a good lawyer and state representative later in life.

As they get older, many male gynics are bothered by their self apparent wimp reactions in stress situations, and – well, it challenges their self evaluation of manhood. In order to counteract this, they may engage in *controlled* dangerous physical activity. After all, as they grow up, they do gain more manly physiques than andrics. Gynics (at the extreme) appear to have been designed by a refrigerator manufacturer. They are large. They are muscular. Working out in the gym with weights will develop very large muscles and a desire to wear tight T-shirts.

Andric males don't mind working out, but only for 10 minutes, and maybe only once every month or so. They have no desire to "look masculine", nor do they have the patience to spend time on machines each day, when they could be active.

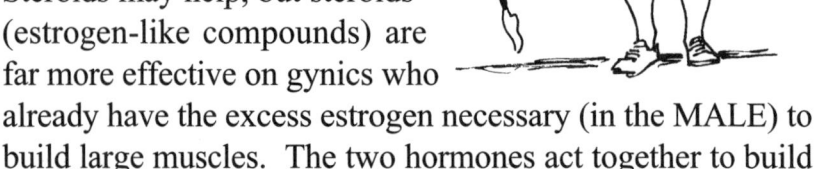

Besides, their muscles will not grow to the proportions that gynics' will even if they try. Steroids may help, but steroids (estrogen-like compounds) are far more effective on gynics who already have the excess estrogen necessary (in the MALE) to build large muscles. The two hormones act together to build large muscle mass. High estrogen levels in females *do not build up muscle mass* as demonstrated by body building females who develop quite *strong* muscles, but they do not have the bulk that males with excess estrogen develop.

There is a mystique of masculinity and danger in being a test-pilot. Who applies? Gynics. Remember, even the daily airline pilots had better be gynics, but for different reasons. Andrics who do fly like the feel of "G's". The pull of gravity. Fast turns, fast speeds, go down as close to the earth as possible, pull up, and let the air horses pull you up into the rough and tumble clouds. Could they be commercial pilots who turn to avoid clouds when possible, who take off gently, who value a touchdown that kisses the runway instead of the Captain Kangaroo style? No way. Keep andrics out of the cockpit.

> *There is a mystique of masculinity and danger in being a test-pilot.*

What Are Your Chances?

Andrics and gynics differ in games of chance. Gynics are willing to let the chips fall where they may after they have calculated the chances of winning. Andrics want more direct control over the situation. Try Vegas. Andrics are more apt (if they gamble at all) to want to throw the dice. They are in control and apt to accept the consequences. Gynics would rather let the house employee shuffle and deal the cards.

Let's take football again. Somebody has to start carrying the football, but who? Only one team starts carrying the ball. Both gynic captains are happy to have the referee flip a coin and will not argue with the decision. Heads or tails. What are your chances? Out of everyone's control. Now, let's invent a really bizarre situation. Say the two teams are composed entirely of andrics. Flip a coin? I doubt it. I can just visualize the referee carrying a card table out onto the field, and watching the two andric captains arm wrestle to determine who gets the ball first. Winner takes all.

Identification – What Are You?
Andric *** or *** Gynic?

Probably a combination of both.

Well, no one is either andric or gynic 100%, but by combining the information offered here, you can glean from physical appearances alone somewhat of a degree that a person might be andric or gynic. And – you do not have to run up to a person and measure arms and legs to find out. At a glance, you have a really good idea of how to talk to either males or females depending on their obvious androgynic body characteristics.

> *No one is 100% andric nor 100% gynic.*

Male or female gynics overall tend to be on the heavy side, and those who are *really* on the heavy side are even more gynic. When weight gain occurs in the gynic, it is gained pretty much all over. In the andric male it is mainly in the belly. The following cartoon regarding an argument between two coaches demonstrates andric and gynic weight and behavior patterns better than any I could possibly describe. Talk about a picture being equal to 1000 words, this one qualifies. Can you tell which is andric, which is gynic, from both the aspects of behavior and weight distribution? I really like this cartoon for its accuracy in demonstrating the Androgynic Factors totally.

Now that men don't wear hats as much as they used to, it is easy to get your first reading on their hormonal influences. Gynic males lose their hair half way between the center of their head and their ears, but retain the center portion forever. This forms a V-shape of hair, or what some people call it a widow's peak. Not sure why. The following drawing demonstrates a *strong* gynic tendency. As gynics age, the path of hair loss increases on the sides, but the hair in front row center will stay there forever. It may thin a bit, but several will remain until the fat lady sings.

When strongly andric males lose their hair, it leaves a totally bare swathe down the center, with fuzzy edges above the ears and around the back of the head. Pictures do better justice than my verbiage.

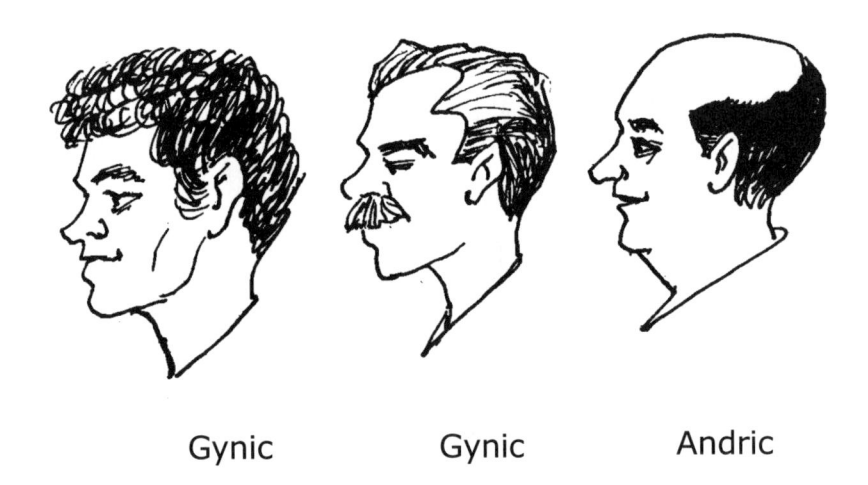

Gynic   Gynic   Andric

Totally bald is a *very* strong andric characteristic. Ever see Yul Brynner? His actions in "The King and I" were quite typically andric. Good acting, for he is not that andric, but portrayed the role well.

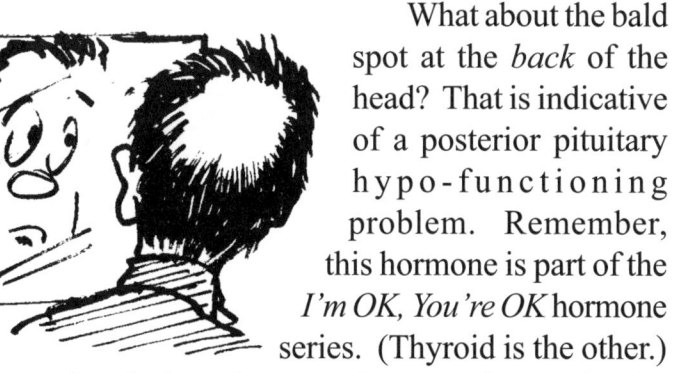

What about the bald spot at the *back* of the head? That is indicative of a posterior pituitary hypo-functioning problem. Remember, this hormone is part of the *I'm OK, You're OK* hormone series. (Thyroid is the other.) Abundant posterior pituitary hormone is present in people who are "always happy". When this baldness appears in the male, the posterior pituitary is hypo-functional (non-abundant), the male feels not so happy with self or others, and small amounts of sugar, alcohol or caffeine will tend to bring out the depression characteristics or the argumentative streaks that are frequent, but *not always* there. Don't take hypo-post pit man out for a three martini lunch if you want to make a sale. As the saying goes, he will have you for lunch.

Strongly gynic males may have a full head of hair, especially snow white hair early in life, and very thick. Think baby-kissing politician. They are affable, very pleasant and exude confidence. They are grandfatherly and incite confidence. They smile easily. They remind you of Santa. They can easily be elected to president of their service club, president of the chamber of commerce, of the business where they work – especially banks. They make great church leaders, foundation heads, anywhere where the *trust factor* is essential.

Gynic

Another instantly identifiable characteristic for differentiation between andric gynic males is facial hair. Gynics are the ones with a moustache or some form of beard.

Generally, the more facial hair, the more gynic. They take great pride in trimming, culturing, shaping, and maintaining the same length. Andrics may try a moustache occasionally, but the time it takes to trim, the effort in matching right side with left side offends their desire to "get on with life". After fussing with trimming a moustache for a few weeks, there comes a day of reckoning in which one swipe eliminates their source of irritation, and they go back to being clean shaven again.

Gynics

This characteristic holds true close to 95% of the time, but beards are still the most dependable first indication before meeting the man. Andrics who grow beards are often the ones who have lost most of their head hair. This may be a compensation.

Sort of reminds me of an old Burma Shave sign I used to see on the way to school:

Andric

"Said Farmer Brown
...who's bald on top
...I wish I could
...rotate the crop."

The more facial hair the male partner has, the more andric that fellow's wife is apt to be. If they are playing the dating game, andric women tend to be more attracted to men with facial hair. In equal and opposite fashion, gynic women are apt

> *The more facial hair the male partner has, the more andric that fellow's wife is apt to be.*

to be more attracted to clean shaven men. Is it the hair? *No.* It is the endocrine pattern attached to that male beard that make the female andric's hormones hum.

If you are a commissioned salesperson approaching a couple with a sale in mind, it is helpful to know that bearded men generally defer to andric wives to make the final decisions. Your sales information should be directed toward instant gratification of bottom line directed information – to the andric wife. Forget the detail. If the bearded one shows interest and asks a question, then he is *really* interested. Most of the time he will just listen, but if he asks a question, immediately change your approach, focus on him (she won't care) and give him the detail leading up to your bottom line presentation eyeball to eyeball. Successful sales people can jump back and forth between an andric and gynic presentation. Keep your weather antenna up for changes in the wind. When the couple goes off together to discuss the decision, he will likely do most of the talking to her, then she will say yes or no. Period. Pass – fail.

Andric

Gynic males generally have far more body hair than andric males.

Gynic males generally have far more body hair than andric males. This may or may not be evident on first introduction. In the summer it is easier to see the hairy arms and chest of the gynic male with a short sleeved shirt. If they are not wearing a tie, you may note hair crawling out their V-necked shirts. If they are wearing a summer sport shirt, it will probably allow a view of lots of masculine looking hairy chest.

Gynic

Andric females by virtue of their additional testosterone may be troubled with more facial, arm and leg hair than their gynic sisters. Especially the upper lip. This becomes a source of irritation to the andric female, for they know they have "masculine" feelings, but do not want any form of masculine appearance. This does not mean they need to undergo a sex change, just that their hormones produce more testosterone than other women.

Another easy-to-spot body shape tattletale is the chin to neck trip. This applies to both males and females. Gynic folks have what is called the Grecian form of neck – starting at the chin. The bottom of the mandible forms a near right angle with the neck. I have the person stand sideways to me to observe this strong indicator.

An andric's chin makes a direct run for the Adam's apple from the tip of the chin forming a slight curve as it goes. If they are overweight, they may have what is called a double chin.

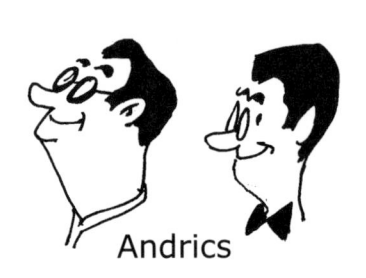

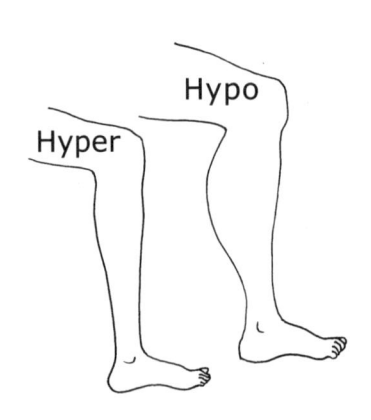

While facing sideways and noting the neck, it is easy to catch sight of the posterior pituitary controlled calf muscles of the leg. Males or females with pronounced musculature in the calf are hypo-posterior pituitary. Remember the sensitivity to sugar, alcohol and caffeine. Their depression will show up easily if they overindulge.

This is a running muscle also. Those with bulky musculature make great sprinters. Blue ribbons for the one hundred dash in high school and college. You bet. How did they do in the mile? Came in last. Distance runners have very thin musculature in the calf. They come in last in the sprint events, yet they can run a mile – three miles – whatever. Which one can do marathon? Certainly not the hypo-post pit person. They can train for years, and still not do well in distance running.

From this information, would you say that jogging is for everyone interested in health? No way. Better find something that requires a burst of energy for the hypo-post pit person.

The following hypo-post pit indicator is another one best observed in a bathing suit, although it can be seen in women with jeans and slacks if you have a keen eye. Page called this indicator the *double dip hip*.

Females instinctively realize that smooth interrupted body curves are the most attractive, so, even by age 4, girls may "strike a pose" imitating pin-up models with one hip turned more toward you and the other turned slightly away. They then push the forward hip even more toward you. This forms the illusion of a smooth hip curve and diminishes the double dip hip.

Watch out for that come-hither smile, for as soon as you give them candy or a cup of coffee, their true self may blossom forth.

When doing an initial examination of a person as a patient, I have them stand and face me to start with. I will usually request that they stand with their hands relaxed at their sides.

Andrics, male or female, have slightly more testosterone, which gives them *greater width* to their shoulders. Simultaneously, it gives them *narrower hips*. They are wedge shaped.

As a result of wider shoulders and narrow hips, their hands have plenty of space to swing when they walk, and the back of their hands will face forward.

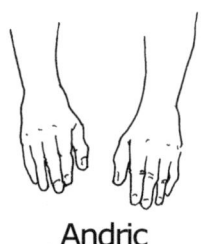

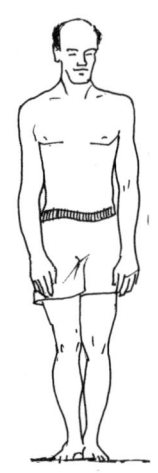

Andric

Gynics have the opposite hormonal developmental influence that results in wider hips and narrower shoulders. If they walked with their hands showing the backs forward, their hands would be constantly bumping into their hips. As a result, their shoulders are slightly rotated such that their hands will be more parallel to their hips and you will see their thumbs lead forward. The backs of their hands will not be visible from the front view. This takes less space, and they can walk without interference from their hips.

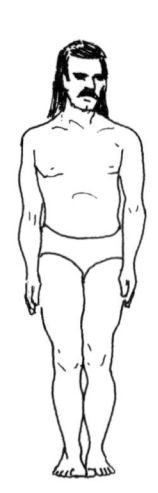

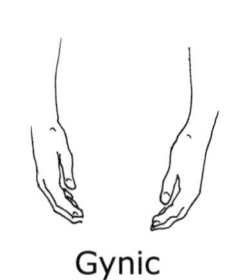

Gynic

Oscillating Hormones

Occasionally you find a person who stands with one hand in the andric position, the other in the gynic position. What kind of an anomaly is this? It does happen. This means that the person can comfortably assume the dominant or the passive role with equal comfort. Males in this category may or may not have facial hair, depending on which hormone is slightly more dominant. Some of these males will wear beards in the winter and not in the summer "to keep their faces warm", but I doubt it. I think it is just oscillating hormones.

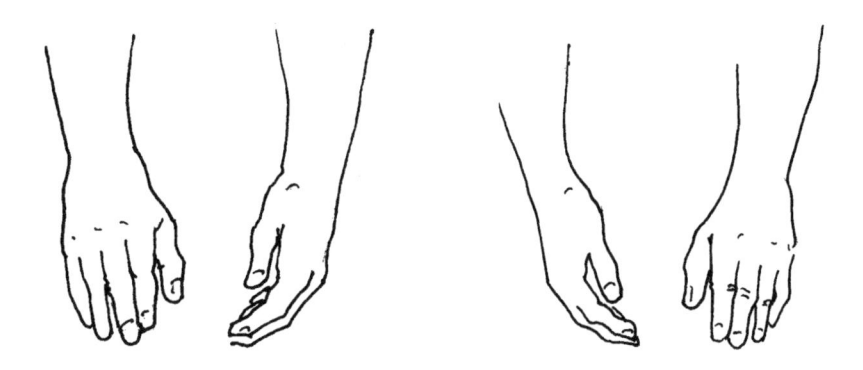

I saw a couple like this last year. Upon noting the differences – not too subtle – very obvious to me, I immediately came to a conclusion.

"You two did not find each other on the first day of dating, I'll bet. It probably took years."

They looked at each other with mutual surprise.

He said, "No, we were thirty four and thirty six when we married. First time for both of us."

"Probably never had more than 3 dates with any one?" I queried.

They looked at each other rather quizzically and nodded.

She said, "We both dated lots of people. We like to be with people, are both pretty outgoing and friendly, but neither of us ever felt anything strong for anyone until we met each other."

He added, "Neither of us thought we would ever get married."

"Until that first date," she chimed in.

He: "Then we both knew. I mean on the first introduction."

"She made your hormones hum?" I suggested.

"Both of us," she answered. "We were married three months later and have really enjoyed being soul mates."

Those magic words. People in that exactly equal and opposite situation really feel that way. You don't have to be perfect matches to be married, but the closer the patterns are to equal and opposite, the more you feel it – forever. It doesn't wear off.

They could throw the ball back and forth every other sentence without feeling like they were being interrupted. Good clue. You can always feel the quiet resentment when an andric interrupts a gynic mate.

Chances of two people with that much andric to gynic oscillation hormones finding each other are not great, but when they do – fasten the Velcro. Ever hear people say of a couple, "I like her, but cannot stand him"? Or the other way around? That will rarely happen to this couple. They can each play either the andric or gynic role, and can adapt so fast that you do not have a chance to dislike either of them. They are a good match for each other, and for any part of human interaction that life situations would place them in.

This is super for personal interaction, but tough from the chemistry balancing point of view. Page would have gone nuts trying to figure out when to switch hormone therapy to match their altering production. Luckily, I found that you don't need as much hormone therapy when the interferences from mercury amalgam fillings and root canals are removed.

Many women wear slacks and jeans more often today, so this next evaluation is easier than it used to be. Again, this is in an office situation, not in a cocktail setting. This is for females only. Doesn't work on males. I have them stand facing me, and take hold of their slacks at about hand level and pull them tight.

Andric   Gynic

If there is a space of about a half an inch to two inches between the thighs, that is an andric characteristic. If the thighs touch all the way down, that is gynic. You can get wrong signals if someone is more than 30 pounds overweight, so it is not always a strong indicator. This is easier to spot on the beach, but andric women in jeans or tight slacks scream andric when walking down the street. They are easy to identify.

You have heard TV admonish you, "do not try this one at home". Well, this one requires discretion. It is the most accurate informant for andric and gynic in the female, but I always have the patient check this for herself and give me a verbal answer. This is another hair line. The pubic hair line. In gynics, the top of the pubic hair line is straight across. In andrics, the top of the pubic hair line is either half moon shaped arching toward the navel, or goes to a peak toward the navel. The peak is the stronger andric indicator.

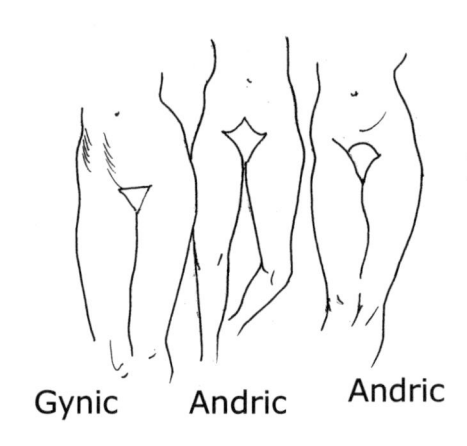

Gynic   Andric   Andric

Living Happily Ever After

is really neat, if you are living with your soul mate, or understand and accept those equal and opposite endocrine patterns of your partner.

"Soul mates" is the end-point target, but that doesn't happen every time. For most of us, there are problems to work out, but there are ways to do that. Understanding and accepting each other's endocrine pattern – *whatever it is* – is good for starters. That eliminates placing blame on others for their weird behavior, just because it doesn't match yours.

> *"Soul mates" is the end-point target, but that doesn't happen every time.*

Be sure to remember that there will be a mid-life reversal of patterns, and be prepared to understand and accept that, too. Shouldn't be too hard, if you are less than 7 years apart in age.

> *Be sure to remember that there will be a mid-life reversal of patterns.*

I was present one time when Page told a couple that they had a very satisfactory sex life. That was not discussed too freely in the 1960's, but Page could ask anything and get honest responses. Yes, they agreed, but how did you know?

"Simple," he answered facing her. "He lets you be the dominant person, and that is what you want. You do not want to be a passive female like our raising leads us to mimic. You control when, and the timing of the events leading up to the actual sexual encounter."

They stared at each other. He continued, as if explaining to me, but they were probably more interested than I, because he had just walked into their bedroom, unseen.

"Their graphs are much closer to equal and opposite than most people. Very fortunate. They have great opportunities for a happy life, and a good sexual relationship is one way to maintain that.

"After all, it is during the actual sex act that you balance each other's hormones. The andric absorbs more estrogen from the gynic, and the gynic absorbs more testosterone from the andric. Doesn't matter which is male or female, hormone exchange is what keeps people's chemistry in balance. With a balanced chemistry, people can handle far more challenge with far less stress. I support sex in a marriage."

If, in that happily ever after phase of your life, you decide to have children, they are the product of the two of you. After pregnancy, it's more than groceries. Genetic engineering takes place daily, based on hormones. Ideally and theoretically, the blueprint of your product (offspring) will not be quite as andric / gynic, nor quite as hypo / hyper as either you or your spouse.

This enables both you and your spouse to watch your kid's behavior, and catch problems early in their development. Why? Because when you were that age, you did the same thing they are doing, and you know why you did it. Ever note that some parents can glance at a child and innately know whether or not he is headed for trouble? They can relate endocrinally and know when to intercede and when to let the child learn on his own. Where do you think "eyes in the back of your head" came from? Kids make your hormones hum, too.

> *What if you want children, but cannot have your own?*

Which brings up another issue. What if you want children, but cannot have your own? (My next book, <u>Please Get Me Pregnant</u>, deals with this.) There is another answer. Adoption. But what are you adopting? Raising kids is difficult and fun simultaneously, but it has its daily challenges you must meet. You can be up to those challenges if you have the energy.

Working parents can be pushed to the limits physically and emotionally, but on days when this is not a factor, you can handle most situations. Children do not come with owner's manuals, but you can usually figure out what to do with your own kid. Your own. Adopted kids are modifications of *their* parents' endocrine imbalances. If – as in the case of adopted kids – they do not fit into your hormone patterns, nor your spouse's, the kids will behave in fashions that you have not the first clue how to handle. You start looking for that owner's manual in books. Like Spock. He was great at predicting tomorrow's growth and development patterns, but no one can tell you how to deal with hormones. Your own kids make your hormones hum with love, but different patterns express love in different ways. Problems. Solvable? Only with great diligence and lots of free way space, love and understanding. Both directions. The kids need to know why they cannot understand their parents, too.

One thing to look forward to is that with maturity – anything over 60 – you will have learned to see life from the perspective of both the andric and the gynic. This is the result of both interacting with other people for many decades, and from undergoing the mid-life reversal so that you, too, have been both andric and gynic. By then, people will say to the andric that you have mellowed. To the gynic they will say that you are now more in charge of your life. In actuality, you can see and accept people better. You are better balanced. Your purpose has been achieved.

Translation from one language to another is difficult at best, due to the subtle actual meanings in one language that do not directly translate into another. When a letter was written hundreds of years prior to being translated, even more errors can occur. I have found one error in an ancient Biblical translation that relates to the theme of this book:

*It's not the "meek" that shall inherit the Earth
— it's the "gynics".*